HORRENDOUS HISTORY

HORRENDOUS HISTORY

by

Amber Grayson

p

This is a Parragon Book
This edition published in 2001

Parragon
Queen Street House
4 Queen Street
Bath BA1 1HE, UK

Produced by Magpie Books, an imprint of
Constable Robinson Limited, London

ISBN 0-75255-790-4

A copy of the British Library Cataloguing-in-Publication Data
is available from the British Library

Printed in China

CONTENTS

The Queen's English

Britain was once a great nation and Queen Victoria ruled over one of the world's largest empires. As each country was conquered so they had to conform to 'the British way', which included learning to speak the language. That's why English is the most widely spoken language in the world today.

Brrr! Brrr!

Lots of things were invented in Victorian times. To name but two, the telephone was invented by Alexander Graham Bell. And the woolly hat, the balaclava, was invented by soldiers during the Crimean War because it was so bloomin' cold at night they needed to cover their faces completely.

As well as being a time of invention, the

Victorian era was a time of great social and economic change. Huge strides were made in technology and, later on, in medicine, as well as in other sciences and the arts.

Extended Family

Queen Victoria was seriously well-connected. By the time she died in 1901, Victoria was related by marriage to all of the major royal families of Europe. That might be why she was nicknamed "the grandmother of Europe".

Vile Victorian Quiz

1) What killed Prince Albert?
2) Which revolution occurred during the Victorian era?
3) Where could you go if you had no home or money?
4) What are The Ashes?
5) Who invented the telephone?

Answers

1) Typhoid.
2) The Industrial Revolution.
3) The workhouse.
4) A trophy given to the winners of the season's Test Matches between England and Australia.
5) Alexander Graham Bell.

CHAPTER TWELVE

Suspicious Spies and the Second World War

It's All in a Name

Adolf Hitler was born in Austria in 1889. His dad was called Alois Schicklgrüber but he changed his surname to Hitler before Adolf was born. If he hadn't, the world might have had quite a different history. Can you imagine millions of people following the Nazi movement if Adolf Schicklgrüber was in charge?

Chocoholic

Hitler wanted to be an architect but he failed his entrance exam for the Vienna Academy of Art. He painted pictures of Viennese buildings and flogged them to make enough money to stay in Vienna for a while and to pay for chocolate cake – his weakness – at the Viennese teahouses.

He fought in the First World War. He was unpopular with his fellow soldiers and was wounded in the leg and later gassed (but not by them).

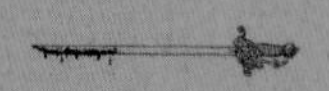

'Allo, 'Allo

During the Second World War, there was huge undercover resistance to the Nazi threat. But people didn't grow up as spies and secret agents. They'd had ordinary jobs before the war. All it took was intelligence, courage, and the ability to think on their feet. (Not much really!)

Secret Address

In Britain, the training for spies and special agents was done at secret addresses in London and at country houses where they learned their undercover work.

British agents were trained how to get into and out of places without anyone finding out, to pick locks and break safes. They were subjected to mock interrogation which meant pretending that they'd been captured by the enemy and learning how to avoid giving away information. One agent joked that she would have made an excellent cat burglar when the war was over.

Tailor Made

The trainee agents were taught how to dress in disguise and were kitted out right down to the tiniest detail. If an English agent was going to pretend to be a French farmworker, for example, there was no point him wearing a suit with a Woolworth's label in it. Special clothes were made up in workshops so that the fabric and style of clothing were exactly right.

Double O Seven

They were given James Bond-style weapons such as silent pistols and gas guns that looked like pens. Women spies used cameras hidden in their handbags. They'd take a picture through a small hole in the bag while pretending to rummage for make-up and stuff.

The French Resistance and the Nazis both used waiters and hotel staff as spies because they could overhear conversations people were having as they ate and drank.

If someone was a great spy but worked for the other side, great efforts would be made to capture them and then "turn them round" so that they spied on their own country.

Radio Ga-Ga

The resistance fighters communicated with each other by special radios which could send and receive coded messages (an improvement on carrier pigeons, which they used in the early days of the war). These were stationed in secret transmitting places, but the Germans were pretty smart at tracking them down. They'd cruise around the place in special detector vans (a bit like the TV licensing people) and try to catch 'em at it. The agents transmitted only short messages to lessen the chances of being tracked down.

Body Painting

Another way of sending a secret message was to write on the agent's body in invisible ink. A special chemical had to be put on the skin in order to see the writing.

Private Post

A letter box hidden in a wall was another place to leave a secret message. A loose brick could be removed to get to the box. Messages were left there for other resistance fighters.

False Alarm

Special agents were brilliant at forging papers. Everywhere you went in wartime Europe you needed proof of who you were because you could be stopped at any time by anyone. It was no use saying, "I'm a French nobody, leave me alone", you had to have the correct documents.

Smoke Screen

It was dangerous for agents to carry any kind of

written message, even if it was in code. If they really needed to do so, one of their tricks was to roll up the piece of paper the coded message was written on, and then insert it into a cigarette with a needle.

Cryptic Conversation

Often agents didn't know the people whom they were supposed to meet to pass on information, so they had to devise a pre-arranged question and answer code so that each agent would know that the other was the right person.

Splitting the Bill

Another trick was to give the spy one half of a banknote, say, 100 francs, and the person they were meeting was given the other half. The two agents would have a description of each other and a pre-arranged meeting place. Each would produce their half of the banknote to prove that they were who they said they were.

Dire Consequences

It all sounds thrilling cloak-and-dagger stuff, the kind of thing you'd watch in a movie on a Sunday afternoon. But for the agents it was a matter of life and death, and one slip could send them into enemy hands and to the torture chamber or firing squad.

Mystery Unveiled

The German coding machine was called Enigma, but the Brits managed to decipher the code, which the Germans thought was unbreakable. The British code-cracking operation was called "Ultra", and the public only heard about it as recently as 1972, years after the Second World War ended. If it wasn't for Ultra, the Allies might never have won the war!

Village Tragedy

People found to be spies or resistance fighters were severely punished. Hitler had a whole village destroyed when one of his SS (special police force) officers was assassinated by two Czech special agents. Although the agents committed suicide, before they could give anything away their names were connected with the village of Lidice. Hitler had all the men shot, the women sent to a concentration camp, and the children to centres elsewhere. The buildings were pulled down and the rubble buried. The village's name was removed from maps.

Also in retaliation, many Czech prisoners were murdered in Nazi jails. Over 2,000 people were killed for the sake of one man's life. Hardly an eye for an eye, or a tooth for a tooth.

The Lesser of Two Evils

Special agents were given cyanide capsules in case they got caught by the Germans. The *Gestapo* (German secret police) were known for their cruelty and some people felt that it was better to kill themselves with a fast-acting poison than have somebody do revolting things to them, and that they wouldn't be able to give anything away if they were dead.

Evacuation
In 1939, during the Second World War, Britain expected to be bombed by Germany, so children were moved out of cities which were likely to be the main targets and sent to stay with strangers in the countryside. This was called *evacuation* and the people who were sent away were called *evacuees.*

Not everyone was happy to suddenly have a bunch of strange children living in their homes, but unless they had a very good reason, people who lived in the "reception areas", as they were called, were forced to take in evacuees or be fined.

As the threat of enemy invasion grew, signposts were removed from roadsides so that if the Germans landed they wouldn't know where they were going!

INTRODUCTION

From the dossers of Ossa, to the glossa of Barbarossa...

There's no beginning and no end to history but it's pretty amazing when you think that about 40,000 years ago the earliest *modern* humans (called *Homo sapiens sapiens*) were living in caves and bashing animals over the head with lumps of stone (and they really *did* have stone beds and cupboards, just like the Flintstones).

Now we're flying to Mars and hanging out in cyber cafes, hunting and gathering information instead of mammoths. This book is about some of the bits in between – not all the boring bits, only the gory, the ghastly and the grim.

CHAPTER ONE

Putrid Pirates

Pirates have been around for a long time, from the days of the ancient Greeks to the present day. The word conjures images of swashbuckling heroes like Captain Hook and Long John Silver, poring over maps of desert islands marked with an X. In reality they were a bunch of nasty, smelly baddies who thought nothing of chopping up innocent people to get at their treasure . . .

Who's the Pirate

Alexander the Great was losing a lot of cash to the pirates or *sea-robbers* of ancient Greece, so he decided to get rid of them. He captured one of the pirate leaders and asked him what he thought he was doing, terrifying all the shipping and nicking all Alexander's stuff.

What could the pirate say to that? He told Alex that he was doing the same thing as him but on a smaller scale. "Since I do it on a small ship I'm called a pirate. Because you do it with a great fleet you're called an emperor." Nice answer, Mr Pirate!

Jules' Revenge

Pirates occasionally got what was coming to them. In ancient Rome, Julius Caesar was taken hostage by pirates and imprisoned until a huge ransom was paid. After his release Julius got even with them – he found the pirates who did it and had them all killed.

Strung Up

The King of Persia showed absolutely no mercy to pirates. His nickname was "Lord of the Shoulders" because whenever he captured a pirate crew he skewered them through the shoulder blades and threaded them all together on a rope.

Down in One!

Vikings were not only pretty good pirates, they were also pretty heavy drinkers. There was a chap nicknamed Stortebeker, which meant "jug or beaker (*beker*) at one swallow", because to get into his gang would-be pirates had to be able to down a load of lager at one go.

Doing the Splits

Islamic pirates were called barbarians by the Europeans and were therefore known as the Barbary corsairs. At the time of the Crusades,

(Wars between Christians and Muslims) at the end of the eleventh century, each side did some horrible things to their prisoners. One of the nasty things Barbary pirates did to the captured Christians was to tie their feet to one ship and their hands to another and for the ships to sail apart. Ouch! It gives a new meaning to being torn in two directions.

The "lucky" ones were captured as slaves and had to row the galley or ship. Often they were starved or beaten to death.

Another bunch of pirates got beheaded in 1573 – all thirty-three one after the other in the market square in Hamburg. The executioner sliced off their heads so quickly that he was sloshing around in their blood. The heads were then displayed as a warning, to discourage any would-be pirates who might be watching.

Sir Pirate

From the sixteenth to the eighteenth century, some pirates were given government permission or licence to steal from enemy ships. These pirates were called *privateers*. All the pirates had to do was to give the king half of their booty. Francis Drake was a privateer and so highly thought of by Queen Elizabeth I that she knighted him (which meant everyone had to call him "Sir" from then on).

There were many "gentlemen" pirates who were well respected and admired. No one seemed to realize that they too were thieves and murderers. One who didn't quite get away with it was Captain Kidd, who was a businessman in New York. He lived at a time when pirates were considered a bad thing. He was sent off on a pirate-hunting expedition but did a few piratey things of his own (persuaded of course by his crew), while he was out hunting them. When he got home he was hanged.

Rid of the Junk(s)

Shap'n'gtzai (or should that be "Sharp and gutsy"?) was a Chinese pirate. One of his fleets, captained by an ex-barber called Chui Apoo, was wiped out by the British navy, who decided that the Chinese pirates were getting too big for their boots.

How did they do it? The Brits cornered the junks (Chinese ships) in the mouth of a river where the Chinese thought they would be safe. But when the tide went out, the junks were positioned so that their guns were pointing at each other and not at their enemy. So the Brits blitzed 'em.

Gold Fever

The *Spanish Main* was the name given to the seas off the north-west coast of the Spanish empire in Central and South America. After the Spanish had conquered countries such as Mexico and Peru, there was a great deal of gold and silver on the ships sailing back to Spain. This had been captured from the Aztecs and the Incas, who were the native

Indian tribes of Mexico and Peru (for more about the Aztecs, see chapter 8/page 163). All that treasure floating around the seas was too great a temptation for pirates everywhere, and soon the route between Spain and the Spanish Main became a major raiding area.

The newly discovered Americas were also known as the New World because, before Christopher Columbus sailed to them, people in Europe thought that there was no land there. Once the rest of the world realized how much treasure Spain was getting out of the New World, they quickly jumped on the bandwagon (well, onto their ships) and went off to grab some gold for themselves.

Pirate crews were often made up of convicts and escaped slaves. They were particularly nasty people who liked nothing better than to torture and then kill anyone who resisted them. And it was good for their reputation to be thought of as seriously mean.

Unholy Smoke!

Blackbeard was the nickname of the legendary pirate Edward Teach. He was much feared and used to set fire to slow-burning tapers under his hat so that he looked even more frightening (not that he needed to). Even so, women seemed to find him attractive – he supposedly had fourteen wives!

Diehard

Blackbeard was so tough that when he eventually met his end he took a long time to die. He was hunted down in 1718 and when trapped was challenged to a duel. He was shot and stabbed twenty-five times before he finally (and literally) hit the deck.

How Offal!

Buccaneers were seventeenth-century pirates who attacked the Spanish in the Caribbean. They got their name from the word "boucan", which was a type of barbecue (don't ask!). They were a gruesome bunch, known for their cruelty. One buccaneer, called L'Ollonais, cut out the heart of a Spanish prisoner and shoved it into the mouth of another. Then he chopped both prisoners into small bits.

Hotlips

Edward Low was an English pirate captain with a similar reputation. He cut off a man's ears and forced him to eat his own lugholes. Captain Low did the same to another man, although this time he cut off his lips and made the speechless man watch as he fried them (how Low can you get?).

Hot Hombres

Another pirate, Rock Brazilliano, spit-roasted two Spanish farmers alive because they wouldn't hand over their pigs to feed the pirate crew. "OK", said Rock, "if you won't let us eat your pigs, we'll eat you instead".

Who Goes There?

All ships would fire a cannon shot to warn another ship to show their flag, or in other words, to say who they were and where they came from. Pirates would cheat by showing the flag of a country friendly with the victim's. Then they'd shout "Heave-to", which meant "Stop!" through a mouth trumpet which was similar to a megaphone.

If the merchant ship wouldn't do as the pirates said, they'd throw a grappling iron at its rigging to pull it close enough to board. They used axes to climb up the wooden sides of the boat and sometimes chucked metal spikes onto the decks so that the sailors (who were usually barefoot) would injure themselves and be out of action.

Femmes Fatales

Sometimes the pirates would pretend to be women and wear broad-brimmed women's hats to fool the other ship. As soon as it had "heaved-to" they would throw off their disguise and jump aboard.

Not-So-Jolly Roger

The Jolly Roger was the name given to a pirate ship's flag. The skull and crossbones wasn't the only emblem. Each pirate ship or fleet had its own design, and black and white weren't the only colours. Other colours like red and yellow were also used. Some flags showed skeletons and hour-glasses (which meant that time was running out for their victims); some used a skull and crossed swords.

Pirate ships were faster than the lumbering merchant ships, which had been built to hold as much cargo as possible, not to speed around on the water. Pirate ships also had shallow hulls, which meant they could get closer to the shore than bigger ships – great for unloading booty in handy caves and for getting away if they were chased.

No Cruise for the Crews

It was a hard life on board. The captain could be as cruel to his crew as he was to the passengers and crew of the captured ships, so there were plenty of lashings. Food was often in short supply and there was usually no water to drink, so pirates drank beer and rum instead. They ate turtles and fish when they could catch them and eggs (which they called cackle-fruit) from live chickens which they could use for meat. It wasn't unknown for them to eat slaves, or even each other, if their ship was becalmed or shipwrecked.

No Broads Aboard

When the pirates did get to shore they often spent all their money on a few evenings of wine, women and song or gambling. Women weren't allowed on board pirate ships. Amazingly enough, there were plenty of women waiting in the ports for the smelly pirates to come ashore, no doubt because of the huge amounts of money they spent.

Although women weren't allowed on board pirate ships, there were some women who disguised themselves as men and became pirates. They had to dress, spit, swear, drink, fight and kill like men.

There was a woman Viking pirate called Alvida who originally became a pirate so that she didn't have to go through with an arranged marriage to a bloke called Prince Alf. Who can blame her for wanting to escape?

Mary Read and Anne Bonny were two other swashbuckling girls. Anne Bonny left her husband for Calico Jack Rackham, who was captain of a pirate ship. She joined Rackham's ship but then fell in love with Mary Read, who was already on board and whom Anne Bonny (and the rest of the crew) thought was a man. It was all very complicated.

The Chinese woman pirate, Ching Shih, who was around in the early 1800s, had 1,800 ships under her command and 75,000 pirates who answered to her.

Another lady sea-robber was Charlotte de Berry, who joined the navy as a man when her husband went to sea. She was assaulted by the captain of the ship and cut off his head in revenge. She then took over the ship and ran it as a pirate vessel.

Paradise Lost

Although a desert island seems like a bit of fantasy out of a chocolate advertisement, it was a severe punishment for pirates who committed a crime while on board their ship. They were allowed a few supplies and a little water, but after that had to fend for themselves. Most died from starvation or disease.

However, there were many exotic tropical islands that were home to pirates. They had many wives and a high standard of living because they were so rich. Some were even able to retire from piracy if they made a good enough "catch" by attacking a treasure-filled vessel.

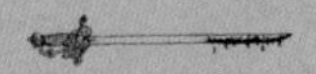

Double Trouble!

A *picaroon* was both a pirate and a slave trader. In the seventeenth and eighteenth centuries, before slavery was abolished in 1833, there were ships full of slaves travelling between Africa and America, and pirates saw the trade as an easy way to make money. They would capture the ships and sell the slaves themselves, or exchange them for goods which they would then sell in another country.

Hang Loose

In Britain, the penalty for being an "illegal" pirate (as opposed to a privateer) was to be "hanged by the neck until *dead*". After that, the bodies of dead pirates were often hung from the *gibbets* (upright posts with an arm coming out of the top), encased in metal skeletons to keep their bones together after their flesh had rotted. This was supposed to put people off becoming pirates – it probably worked quite well!

Steam Cleaned

Piracy was eventually wiped out by the late nineteenth century, when steamships were invented, and the seas became safe again. Steamships could obviously travel without wind and so they could chase the pirate ships and destroy them.

Putrid Pirates Quiz

1) What was a privateer?
2) What was the Spanish Main?
3) What was a picaroon?
4) Who were the Barbary corsairs?
5) What command ordered a ship to come to a halt?

Answers

1) A pirate who had a licence to rob ships.
2) The name given to the seas off the north-west coast of the Spanish empire in Central and South America.
3) A pirate and slave trader.
4) The Islamic pirates of the southern Mediterranean.
5) "Heave-to!"

CHAPTER TWO

Churlish Chinese

The ancient Chinese called their country *Zhongguo*, which means Middle Kingdom, because they believed that they were the centre of civilization. They had a Stone Age around 8000 BC–2500 BC, after which they became a bit more civilized and haven't stopped being civilized since.

We hear all the time about different Chinese dynasties, like the Qin, Han, Tang, Song, Ming, etc. What exactly was a dynasty?

A dynasty was a line of rulers from the same family. The dynasty changed when the family line ran out (no more sons to take over the throne) or when the emperor was overthrown, either by another Chinese ruler or by someone from another country.

The first dynasty was the Xia Dynasty, which was founded in 2100 BC. It went on for 500

years, so they were either doing a good job or they were so nasty that people didn't dare get rid of them.

Consult the Bone!

After Xia came Shang. In the Shang Dynasty fortune-telling was popular. One of the ways of doing this was by cracking the bone from an animal (a dead one) or sometimes the shell of a tortoise and reading the fractures – a bit like reading tea leaves in the bottom of a cup. Then the fortune-teller would write what he saw in the cracks (that is, what the cracks were supposed to mean) on the bone or shell. These were known as *oracle* bones.

Potent Powder

Years later, when these bones with characters scratched all over them were found, people thought they were magic dragons' bones. They ground them up and used them in medicines, believing that these magic bones would make them better.

Pieces of China

In 1122 BC, the Zhou ruler, Wu (it's all true!), beat the Shang emperor and took over, starting the Western Zhou Dynasty, which was followed by the Eastern one.

After that time China was divided up into lots of different states and they were always scrapping with each other. In 221 BC all the states were centralized, which meant that they were all brought under one ruler. China therefore became an *empire* and was known as *Imperial* China.

Not Dead and Buried

Qin Shi Huangdi was the man who made China into an empire. He was called the *First Emperor* and he came to the throne at the age of nine. Unfortunately he became a bit of a horror. One

of the things he did was to burn most of the books and papers that people had written in the past, because he wanted things to be done his way and didn't want anyone else influencing the present. As for people who wrote books, he just buried them alive.

Qin Shi Huangdi was a bit of a big shot and had a tomb made for himself which took 700,000 people more than thirty-six years to build. By the time they'd finished they were probably hoping he'd hurry up and get in it!

Model Army

In 1974 the First Emperor's tomb was discovered, together with several thousand life-sized models of soldiers who were guarding it. The clay soldiers are called the *Terracotta Army* and have been displayed all over the world. Life-sized models of horses and chariots were also found. These were supposed to protect Qin Shi Huangdi from evil spirits. The fact that he had so many must have meant he had a guilty conscience!

Big Bang

Four years after Qin Shi Huangdi died the Qin Dynasty was chucked out and Han took over. Han Gaozu was a minor civil servant, whose real name was Liu Bang. He thought Qin Shi Huangdi was making a bit of a mess running the country and that he could do better. He began the Han Dynasty and was a bit kinder than the First Emperor.

Order of Merit

In Imperial China there was a very definite order of importance or *hierarchy* for each type of person, which went like this:

The Emperor came first of course.

The nobles and scholars were second in importance and were known as the *Shi*.

Next came the peasant farmers, known as the *Nong*.

After that were the *Gong*, or craftworkers, followed lastly by the merchants and traders, called the *Shang*.

All you have to remember is: *Shi, Nong, Gong, Shang*. Easy.

The Nong were second in importance to the nobles and scholars, because, even though they had a very silly name, everyone thought farming was very important (quite right too!). The Shang came at the bottom, because even though some of them were fabulously rich, the farmers, who were usually skint, were much more highly thought of. Which goes to show that it's not what you *know* that counts, it's what you *hoe*.

Fruitful Advice

A *mandarin* isn't only a type of orange, it was also the name given to an adviser to the emperor. Around 2,000 years ago, there were fifty-nine and a half million people in China, so the emperor couldn't rule everyone by himself – he needed a lot of advisers and officials.

The emperor ruled very strictly and if you didn't do as you were told, you'd probably be cut in half or torn apart, so most people decided to behave themselves (well, you would, wouldn't you?)

The poor old peasants wore cotton trousers and tunics, and a bit of sheepskin to keep them half warm in the winter, while the nobles wore elaborate silk costumes embroidered with fantastic designs in gorgeous colours. And nobody was allowed to wear the colour yellow except for the emperor.

Slinky Silk

Chinese silk – the Chinese called it *si* – was the best in the world. The caterpillars of a certain type of moth were used. Known as silkworms, these caterpillars needed to be fed on mulberry

leaves (and indeed still are). Then they spun a protective outer casing called a *cocoon*. After the silkworm had finished spinning, the cocoon was plunged into boiling water and the thin web or *filament* was unravelled. Sometimes this could be as long as a kilometre (over half a mile). It was then woven into silk cloth. The Chinese kept their knowledge of silkmaking a secret, until some silkworms were smuggled to the West by some greedy monks!

Building Sites

In 400 BC the Chinese began to build the Grand Canal, which is still in use today. It links the Yellow River with the Yangtze River and is nearly 1,800 kilometres (1,125 miles) long. It only took around a thousand years to build!

The Great Wall of China was begun at the same time as the Grand Canal. It is 4,000 kilometres (2,500 miles) long and was built over a period of around 2,000 years – each emperor would add a bit more. It was used as a line of defence as well as a route because the top was wide enough to travel on. Even today it is the only man-made object that can be seen from an orbiting spacecraft.

Both these building projects are amazing feats when you consider that the ancient Chinese had none of the heavy earth-moving machinery that is in use today. And they show that the ancient Chinese were very progressive. They would carry on the work of the last emperor or dynasty, even if they didn't like it, rather than destroying everything the last one had done so they could rebuild it and take the credit.

Weight of Responsibility

The emperor believed he was descended from the gods and that he was the Son of Heaven. Occasionally he'd go to a religious festival or two and do lots of *rituals* (a type of ceremony) in the temples and in his palace because it was the done thing for an emperor. He also did a lot of ordering people around because that was another thing that emperors were expected to do, and there were a lot of people to do it to.

Whenever he went out and about on his imperial business, the emperor was usually

carried in a chair known as a litter. Some of the temples where he prayed or made sacrifices were right at the top of steep-sided mountains – not much fun for the people who were carrying him.

Road to Riches

In 112 BC China began trading with Europe and Asia, and what is known as the *Silk Road* trading route was set up. Ancient China was self-sufficient, which means that the people produced almost everything they needed, but Europe and Asia wanted a lot of the stuff that the Chinese had to offer, so China became very rich and powerful.

A rich noble or merchant would have a home in town and a big place in the country, with plenty of servants to do the dirty work. The sleeves on the silk gowns of the nobles and their wives were enormous to show that they were rich and important enough not to have to do anything grubby. They grew their fingernails very, very long for the same reason, and to prove that they never had to do the washing-up.

Golden Years

In the eighth century AD, China became a superpower (although they weren't known by that name in those days) and there was what is known as a *golden age* of Chinese arts and literature. This means that they produced some really good books, poetry, paintings, music and suchlike. The most important thing to the Chinese was painting, the more realistic and natural-looking the better. They did lots of pictures of mountains and lakes because they were symbols of the elements, as well as looking nice.

Cool Caskets

The ancient Chinese (the wealthy ones) had a kind of air-conditioning, consisting of beautiful caskets with decorative grids on top, which held lumps of ice. Many of these caskets placed around the room would keep it cool during the long hot summers. They were keen on keeping cool and having lots of nice things to look at so, as well as containing works of art, most of the nobles' houses had elaborate gardens with pools, waterfalls, fruit trees and scented flowers.

New Ideas

The Chinese were, and still are, great inventors. This is how good they were: they invented printing around 600 AD although Europe didn't learn how to print until about 800 years later! One of the few things the Chinese hadn't thought of was clockwork goods. These, when they were imported from the West, fascinated the Chinese.

The Chinese also invented: gunpowder, which

they used in fireworks and later as ammunition; the seismograph (for detecting earth tremors); the magnetic compass, paper, and kites, plus a host of other things – and they're still at it!

Back to Front

Chinese writing reads from right to left, the opposite way to the way we do it in the West. Chinese words are made up of symbols or simple pictures which are called *characters*. There are over 40,000 characters made from eleven basic brush strokes. The writing or painting of the characters is called *calligraphy* and is extremely difficult to do because the *calligrapher* has to keep the brush upright and mustn't let his wrist rest on the table.

Tough Love

If you were a kid, life was harsh at home in ancient China. Even if you weren't a peasant slogging your socks off in the fields, you were still brought up very strictly. The father was the head of the household and everyone had to obey him. Sometimes he had a second wife or concubine – so Chinese children might have two or more mothers to boss them about! Marriages were arranged by the parents, whether or not the bride and groom liked each other.

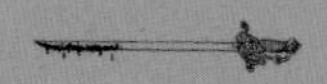

If it Moves . . .

The Chinese have grown rice for centuries. Growing rice involves planting the seedlings in a very soggy field, known as a paddy field, and draining it before the harvest. But the ancient Chinese didn't just eat rice; the wealthy ate delicious things like noodles and dumplings, usually steamed and flavoured with chilli, garlic, ginger, and sesame. The meat course needed a second look though, because as well as the usual pork, chicken and so on, they ate animals like turtle, bear (or just bear paws!), dog, and monkey. The ancient Chinese

had no qualms about eating whatever was available.

Believe it or Not!

The Chinese had three religions. *Confucianism* and *Daoism* are actually *philosophies*, which means that they are based on ideas. The people who thought up the ideas were worshipped in the same way as gods. The third religion was *Buddhism*, which came along a bit later.

Confucius was born in 551 BC and his real name was Kong Fuzi -Confucius is the Latin version of his name. He wrote a book called *Analects*, which means "Sayings".

According to Confucius, everybody should know their place and respect everyone else. Children should obey their parents (and bow to them every time they saw them); wives had to obey their husbands and everybody had to obey the emperor, of course.

This was great if you were born an emperor or a noble, but if you were born poor and had to work in the fields or down the mines for peanuts, old Kong Fuzi's sayings became less attractive. All the emperors followed the teachings of Confucius (well they would, wouldn't they?), but the peasants weren't so sure. There were many revolts and uprisings over the centuries, because the peasants really did have a raw deal.

Daoism was supposedly founded in 604 BC by a chap called Lao Zi, who was a court librarian. However, nobody seems to know much about him so perhaps he was invented. *Dao* means "the way" and it's all about being in harmony with nature and with your surroundings.

Buddhism came from India in about AD 80. Buddha said that all the wrongs of the world, and all the suffering and pain that go on, are caused by desire. Buddhists believed (and still do) that we relive our lives until we stop wanting material things. So next time you just *have* to have those shoes or that CD, just think you

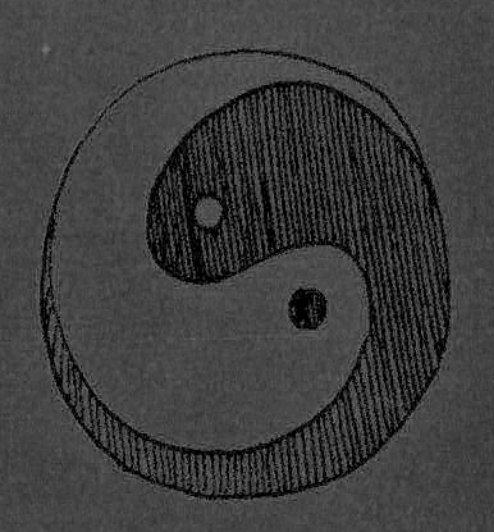

THE YIN AND YANG SYMBOL

might have to live yet another life to pay for it (the desire that is, not the object of it).

Yin and Yang

The ancient Chinese believed in Yin and Yang, seen as the two great energy sources. Yin is female and stands for dark, quiet, softness, and so on, while the male Yang is represented by light, noise, and hardness. Life should consist of a balance of the two in order to achieve health, wealth, and happiness. Chinese people still believe this today, and the principles of Yin and Yang have been taken up by many people the Western world.

Martial Arts

Wu shu isn't a sneeze – it's the Chinese name for *martial arts*, a discipline of the mind as well as the body. This combines the gentle principles of the Buddhist and Daoist religions – harmony, peace, respect – with the "Kill 'em before they kill you" mentality of the fighting warrior. It was a great combination, and lots of the stuff we do in our leisure time in the West like tai chi, chi gung and so on comes from these ancient Chinese martial arts.

What's the Point?

Acupuncture has been around since about 2700 BC. It's the science of piercing the body in certain places with very thin needles to help its natural energy, or *qi* (we pronounce it "chi"), to flow properly. It is still widely used in Chinese medicine, and is also practised in Western countries.

Power Towers

Pagodas are tall, pointed buildings, sometimes several storeys high. They were usually built on holy sites and were, and still are, supposed to bring good luck and energy to the area around them.

Afterlife Luggage

The ancient Chinese believed in life after death. Servants, horses and dogs were sometimes killed to go into the tomb of a dead person, together with favourite possessions, jewels, clothes, food, cooking pots, the kitchen sink – anything that the deceased might need in their next life.

Well Dressed!

They also dressed up their dead. One ancient Chinese woman whose grave was found quite recently was very well preserved. She was wearing twenty layers of clothes and was encased in four coffins!

White is the colour of mourning in China. When someone in the family died, the children had to wear white clothes for three years.

Bound to Hurt

Chinese men thought women with tiny feet were the business or, at least, very glamorous. In order to keep their feet small, girls would have their feet bent almost in two and bound very tightly so that the bones broke and the toes curled under, stunting the growth of the foot.

They called them "lily feet", but there was nothing flower-like about them. They often smelled really bad because the skin couldn't breathe properly.

Foot binding caused most women to hobble – some could hardly walk at all, they were in such agony. They wore little silk socks in bed and never showed their naked feet to their husbands because, although the feet looked OK in the dainty little slippers women wore, they didn't look too pretty in the flesh! The amazing thing is that foot binding was only banned in 1926.

Noble Pursuits

The ancient Chinese liked playing polo, and it was very popular among noblewomen. The question is, how did they keep their bound feet from falling out of the stirrups? Gambling was also big in China – they'd gamble on anything: card and dice games, animal fights, whether it was going to rain the next day . . .

An Impressive Empress

Towards the end of the seventh century AD, the emperor Tang Gaozong got rid of his wife and replaced her with Wu, his *concubine* (girlfriend or second wife). When the emperor became ill, Wu did what was unheard of for a woman and took over the country, making herself empress. This caused shock and horror all round: it was hard enough to wake up and find someone completely different in charge, but for it to be a woman . . .! The men of the court tried to stop her but she got her own way. Well won, Wu!

Make Your Mind Up!

Did you know that Beijing used to be called Peking? Before that, during the time of the Mongols, it was called Khanbalik.

Labour of Love

The Imperial Palace in Beijing was built between 1407 and 1420 by Emperor Yongle. He didn't do it himself of course, because his fingernails were too long, but he did get hundreds of thousands of workers to build it.

The Imperial Palace was called the Forbidden City because the ordinary man on the street wasn't allowed to go near it – probably for fear that he would be made restless with envy if he saw the luxury that surrounded the emperor. It was huge and beautiful, had gardens and courtyards and moats, and was more fantastic than ordinary people could believe. During the Ming Dynasty, the Imperial Palace employed 9,000 maids together with thousands of other servants.

Manchu Rule

In 1644, Ming rule was overthrown by the Manchu invasion and the Qing Dynasty began. Among other things, men now had to wear a long ponytail.

Pinkie Nails

The rich grew the nails of their little fingers really long – perhaps for picking their noble snouts? They had to wear nailguards to stop them breaking off (the nails, not the noses).

Sartorial Dictate

The emperor told his court precisely how to behave and even what colour clothes to wear (maybe so they didn't clash with him!).

Chinese Takeaway

In the early nineteenth century, foreign powers

realized what a rich source of treasures China was, and started to try to boss the Chinese around and take over their trade. In 1842 Hong Kong was leased to Britain. It was finally returned to China in 1997.

Boat to Nowhere

In 1862, Empress Dowager Cixi became regent, meaning that she was in charge. She used money meant for the Chinese navy to have a marble model of a Mississippi paddle steamer built at her Summer Palace. Evidently she thought that a full-size marble boat which never went anywhere was much more useful than a navy.

Last in Line

The last emperor of China was only a little boy when he came to the throne in 1908. He was called Puyi (on account of the smell of his nappies?). He only lasted four years because China then became a republic and Puyi had to abdicate (get off the throne fast before he got his head chopped off). He later went to part of China that had been invaded by Japan. The Japanese made him Emperor of this region, for which he was imprisoned after the Second World War. Finally he was pardoned and ended his days as an ordinary citizen, working in a garden – a real riches to rags story.

Churlish Chinese Quiz

1) What did the ancient Chinese call their country?
2) What is a *dynasty*?
3) What were *oracle* bones?
4) What did the Chinese call lily feet?
5) What is *Wu shu*?

Answers

1) Zhongguo, or Middle Kingdom.
2) A line of rulers from one family.
3) Animal bones with messages foretelling the future.
4) Feet that had their growth stunted by binding.
5) The name for Chinese martial arts.

CHAPTER THREE

Egotistical Egyptians

The ancient Egyptian civilization lasted for almost 3,000 years and made Egypt one of the richest countries in the world. The ancient Egyptians were ruled by *pharaohs*, who were their kings. The people believed that their pharaoh was a descendant of the gods and if they didn't obey him, or even look after him properly, then things would go wrong for them.

The pharaohs had complicated names like Nebhepetra, Mentuhotpe and Tutankhamun (who everyone's heard of because his tomb was discovered in 1922). Tutankhamun was only eight when he became pharaoh, which is pretty young to have all that responsibility. There was Hatshepsut, who was a woman and not really supposed to be a pharaoh. She was the mother of the ten-year-old pharaoh but she took charge. Statues and drawings of her show her wearing men's clothes and a beard!

Dissolution of the Temples

The pharaoh Akhenaten did the same thing as Henry VIII was to do centuries after him: he decided that the priests had too much money and too much say in what was going on, so he took it all away from them.

Big Ram

Ramesses II was the pharaoh who built the most and the biggest buildings because at the time of his rule the Egyptian empire was huge and very, very rich from all the taxes that they charged.

Martian Brickies

Some of the pyramids are so enormous that in the past (and even now, to some extent) people believed that they were built by beings from outer space. Now there is evidence to suggest that the Egyptians could have built the pyramids because they had superb mathematical and building skills. The slabs of stone which make up the sides of the pyramids fit together so well that you couldn't fit a hair in between. But nobody really knows how they actually did it, so perhaps extraterrestrials did lend a hand (or six!).

Windy Wages

The workers who built the pyramids were sometimes paid in garlic and radishes to keep their stomachs healthy. Parp! You'd think they'd demand hard cash for lumping all those stones around.

Wash 'n' Go

The pharaoh would be washed each day by women from his *harem* – the female members of his circle, who were usually his wives and girlfriends. They had to give the smelly old pharaoh a scrub down before he did his daily job of running the empire.

Bald Statement

Priests shaved every day – not just their beards,

but their heads and bodies as well. Priests also breathed in perfumed smoke called incense to bring them closer to their gods.

Neat Pleat

The ancient Egyptians liked to look as glamorous as possible. The women wore long linen dresses, sometimes pleated (which was something the Egyptians invented), and the men wore a kind of cotton skirt. And they all wore make-up, even the men!

Waxy Wigs

It wasn't only the priests who shaved their heads – some of the ordinary people did too. Then they'd wear wigs. (Why bother to shave in the first place?) After that, the women would put blobs of waxy perfume on top of their heads to melt in the sun and make them smell fabulous.

Animal Idols

The ancient Egyptians worshipped animals as gods. The goddess of joy and motherhood was called Bastet and she looked like a cat. She was very popular because, although she had

only one festival a year, it turned into a bit of a party. Among the other Egyptian gods, Sobek was a crocodile, Khnum had a ram's head, Anubis had a dog's head, and Thoth was a man with a bird's head on his shoulders. When a sacred animal died it was *mummified* (specially treated to preserve its body).

Fortuitous Floods

The Egyptians planted their food crops on the banks of the River Nile. If it wasn't for the fact that the Nile flooded every year, there would have been no civilization there at all. After the flood waters had receded (died down), they left behind a thick muddy ooze which was very fertile. Seeds were sown into this and herds of animals would be driven behind the sowers to trample the seeds into the soil, making a very efficient ploughing machine.

Fun and Games

Although the Egyptians worked hard, they didn't want to end up too stressed so they played hard as well. They had loads of festivals and games and sports and liked to relax with plenty of music and dancing. It was usually the girls who danced – with not very much on – and they'd do acrobatics and gymnastics as well.

Lost Language

Hieroglyphs are what the ancient Egyptians used for writing. They are drawings or inscriptions which make up words or sentences. For centuries, no one knew what the little pictures and inscriptions on walls and caskets meant. Then, in 1799, the *Rosetta Stone* was discovered. This stone had a story both in hieroglyphs and in Greek (which people could understand) so from that they eventually worked out the meaning of all 750 characters.

Swap Shop

At first the Egyptians didn't use money to buy things, they just swapped what they wanted for something they had. Eventually they used *debens*, which were copper weights. Each article or product had a value in debens and so they swapped for a fixed price.

Holy Island

Elephantine isn't the size of your bottom, it was a sacred island in the River Nile which had a temple on it where people worshipped for 3,000 years (that's a very long church service!).

Feeling Empty Inside

The Egyptians believed that after they died they had a chance to live another life, so they *embalmed* dead bodies so that they didn't decompose (rot). It was a bit of a palaver and took ages to do. They took all the insides out (except the heart), filled the body with scented leaves and bits of cloth, then sewed it up. They dried out all the other bits like the liver, stomach, lungs, and intestines, and put them into jars which went into the tomb with the body – just in case they needed them again!

Wrap Up!

Then the body was covered in salt crystals (called *natron*) for about three months, which dried it out completely and made sure that it didn't go off. After that it was rubbed with perfumed oil and wrapped in miles and miles of bandages. Bits of jewellery, called *amulets*, were tucked in between the layers to ward off evil spirits. A mask which was painted to look like the person's face was placed on top and the body was put into a coffin. Only then was it ready for the funeral.

Buried Treasure

The Egyptians made funky jewellery out of gold and semi-precious stones. But it was no good hoping that your great aunt Cleo would leave you her trinkets – they were buried with her when she died so she could use them in the afterlife.

Eye Plug

If an ancient Egyptian had trouble with his eyes, the doctor would grind up the eye of a pig with a few other bits and pieces and stick it in the patient's *ear*! Weird or what?

Conquered at Last

The Egyptians had plenty of enemies and lots of people wanted to conquer them. Mostly their enemies failed because the ancient Egyptians were brilliant in battle, but in 525 BC the Persians finally got them. The King of Persia wasn't very nice to them and wouldn't let the Egyptians worship their gods or do all the other things that were important to them, and which they'd been doing for hundreds of years.

Change of Lifestyle

Then, in 332 BC, Alexander the Great came from Greece and captured Egypt from the Persians. Slowly, the Egyptians began to take on the Greek way of life, and the ancient Egyptian culture and writing began to disappear.

No Imagination

Alexander's general, Ptolemy, took over when Alexander died and for a period of almost 250 years Egypt was ruled by the general's descendants, known as the Ptolemies. There were fourteen pharaohs, all called Ptolemy, but the queens had a bit of variety: they were called either Cleopatra or Arsinoe (well, it could have been worse).

Surgical Incision

The Ptolemaic period was a time of, merging of the arts and sciences of two of the greatest civilizations, the Egyptian and the Greek. There were great improvements in medicine, partly owing to Ptolemy III letting Erasistratus, his doctor, practise his surgical skills and do some nasty experiments on criminals who had been given the death sentence.

Keep it in the Family

The fourth Ptolemy (Ptolemy IV, believe it or not) killed his father so that he himself could become pharaoh. The Ptolemies were a bloodthirsty bunch: Ptolemy VIII went on to murder his wife as well as his nephew.

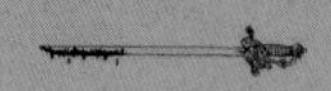

All of a slither

Cleopatra VII was the last queen of Egypt. She became queen by killing off her brother in 44 BC (she was a Ptolemy – what can you expect?). She was supposedly gorgeous-looking and a pretty good ruler too. She was married to a Roman, Mark Antony. Unfortunately, that didn't help her much, and she lost a fight with the Romans in 31 BC, after which Egypt became a Roman province. Cleopatra committed suicide by allowing poisonous snakes called *asps* to bite her.

In Enemy Hands

It wasn't good for the Egyptians to be ruled by the Romans. They were allowed to worship their gods but they had to pay loads of money to the Romans in taxes. They lived in occupied territory, that is to say that Roman soldiers were always around somewhere, so it wasn't exactly relaxing being an Egyptian in those times.

End of an Era

Slowly the ancient traditions died out. In AD 391 the Romans closed most of the Egyptian temples, and people lost the ability to read hieroglyphs altogether. Ancient Egypt had disappeared.

Egotistical Egyptians Quiz

1) What were hieroglyphs?
2) What was a deben?
3) What was embalming?
4) Which Greek conquered Egypt?
5) When did the Romans take Egypt from the Greeks?

Answers

1) Pictures of characters which made up early Egyptian writing.
2) A copper weight, used instead of coins.
3) Wrapping dead bodies in tight layers of cloth to preserve them.
4) Alexander the Great.
5) In 31 BC.

CHAPTER FOUR

Gargantuan Greeks

The ancient Greeks had everything: good looks, intelligence, great bodies. They were good at art, philosophy, mathematics, painting, sculpture, pottery, dance, and sport. Don't you hate them already?

The first Greek civilization began with the Minoans on the island of Crete. They'd been there since about 6000 BC but reached the peak of their civilization between 2100 BC and 1500 BC. The Minoans were rich and peaceful (which was rare), and built many beautiful palaces.

Girl Power!
The Minoans were taken over by the Mycenaeans around 1500 BC. The Mycenaeans worshipped goddesses and mere gods (male) seemed to be much less important to them.

Out of Line

The Minoans had learned how to write in order to keep records of all the goods they stored. This script is now called *Linear A* and nobody has yet worked out how to decipher it! The Minoans taught the Mycenaeans how to write and they fiddled around with Linear A until they produced their own script, which is known as *Linear B*. This has been deciphered but the writing that has been translated has turned out to be very boring – just long lists of goods and people's names.

LINEAR B

Shopping list
½ pound cheese
1 dozen eggs
a jar of honey
a sliced loaf

TRANSLATION

The Wooden Horse

When famine or earthquake struck, the Mycenaeans would attack the neighbouring countries to steal what they needed. But it wasn't lack of food that caused the Trojan War in around 1250 BC – it was a woman, or rather, two men fighting over the same woman.

Helen of Sparta was so beautiful that all the Greek kings wanted to marry her. Helen eventually married Menelaus, the brother of King Agamemnon of Mycenae.

However, Aphrodite, the Greek goddess of love, made Helen fall in love with a chap called Paris, who was a Trojan. She left her husband and went off with Paris to Troy. Agamemnon was so furious that his brother's wife had sloped off with another bloke that he and the Greek army tried for ten years to get into the walled city of Troy to get her back, but with

no luck. Finally they thought up a cunning plan.

The Greeks built a huge wooden horse, left it outside the city, and went away. After they'd gone, the Trojans saw the horse, scratched their heads, and then wheeled it inside the city walls. Unfortunately for them, the horse was hollow and full of Greek soldiers. They climbed out during the night and opened the city gates to let in the rest of the army, which had sneaked back and was waiting outside. They attacked the sleeping city, killed all the men, and made the women and children slaves.

True or False?

The Trojan Horse story was written by the blind Greek poet, Homer. At first it was thought to be just a load of twaddle. However, a nineteenth-century German explorer believed completely in the story and set off to find the city of Troy. He found the remains of a city which might have been Troy in what is now Turkey, so who knows, it might have been true after all.

Unbelievable Myth

Homer also wrote about the hero Odysseus who, on his way back from the Trojan War, met a *Cyclops* (a man-eating giant with only one eye in the middle of his forehead) called Polyphemus.

Polyphemus trapped Odysseus and his men in his cave and began to eat them alive. Odysseus offered the giant some wine and, when he was flat out in a drunken stupor, stuck a red-hot stake into his one eye and blinded him so that they could all escape.

That story is a bit more believable, isn't it?

Drop in Standards

Greece went through a bit of a bad patch for about 300 years, from 1100 BC to 800 BC, in a period known as the *Dark Ages*. All their skills went downhill, their population decreased, and they lived in mud huts, which they wouldn't have been seen dead in before!

Easy as ABC

The Greeks forgot how to write during the Dark Ages, and it was only when they started trading with the Phoenicians, in around 800 BC, that they started to jot things down again. Trouble was, the Phoenician alphabet contained no vowels. (Hw cld thy wrt lk tht?) The Greeks added extra signs for the vowels and bingo, the forerunner of the alphabet we use today was born.

The Purple Men

The Phoenicians came from what is now Lebanon. Their name comes from the Greek word *Phoinikes*, which means "purple men", because they produced a purple dye.

Aristos and Underdogs

In ancient Greece there were only free men or slaves. The slaves were prisoners of war or foreign people bought from slave traders. From 800 BC Greece was divided into states owned by the *aristoi*, which means "the best people" and is where the word *aristocrat* comes from. The aristoi were very rich and powerful and they were the only people allowed to have a say in how the state was governed. This was great for them but bad for the people not born into the right class.

Harsh Punishment

Did you know that the word *tyrant* means "ruler"? Greece went through a stage of having a lot of tyrants in charge, one after the other. They could do what they wanted without consulting anyone. Draco was a one of these tyrants and he devised a new set of rules which were really strict. During his rule, it was quite normal to be killed for stealing a loaf of bread.

Nowadays, when stiff punishments are given, or strict rules made, they are said to be *Draconian*.

Root Cause

A lot of the words which make up many European languages have roots in Greek (as well as Roman) words. The word *ostracize*, which means "to banish", comes from the ancient Greeks. When people wanted to get rid of a politician they would write his name on a piece of pottery called an *ostrakon*. If more than 6,000 ostrakons were counted, the politician had to leave Athens for nine years. It's a shame that we can't do a similar thing nowadays!

Public Opinion

In about 500 BC the Greeks had had enough of being pushed around by the aristocracy and so they invented *democracy*. This allowed men (women had no say in public life – the ancient Greeks weren't that advanced!) to vote for a leader and to have a say in how the country or state was to be governed. That's the theory, anyway.

Feeling Philosophical

The Greeks were very hot on philosophy. The word philosophy in Greek means "love of wisdom". The philosophers Socrates, Plato, and Aristotle would sit around in the sun, discussing the meaning of life, which is a nice job if you can get it.

However, Socrates became a bit of a threat to

the people in charge because he was cleverer than they were. In 399 BC he was accused of corrupting young people (well, they had to have an excuse, didn't they?). Socrates was forced to commit suicide by drinking poison.

Unused Hypotenuse

Pythagoras was a mathematician and philosopher. Unfortunately he wasn't poisoned and had time to write Pythagoras' theorem which, for some reason, we all have to learn by heart.

No Post-Mortem

Although they were great philosophers and seemed to know a lot about the mind, the ancient Greeks weren't so good on the body. They didn't believe in cutting up the dead, so doctors didn't know very much about what made people ill or how the body worked.

Medical Curse

Hippocrates was one of the great Greek doctors, and it was from him that the term *Hippocratic* oath came. For many centuries, doctors had to swear the Hippocratic oath before they could practise medicine. This no longer happens, but the principles of modern medicine are still based on the ideas of Hippocrates.

School Run

Boys were sent to school from around the age of seven. If you were the son of noble (therefore rich) parents, you'd have a slave, called a *paidogogos*, to take you to school and to sit and look after you when you were there (and to eat your school dinner for you if you were really lucky).

Different for Girls

Girls had to stay at behind and learn to do spinney-weavey stuff, and how to run a home.

Then they'd be married off at the age of thirteen or so, usually to older men who were chosen for them by their fathers.

Sporting Matters

Boys were taught all the usual stuff, as well as a lot of sports like athletics and wrestling, all of which was done in the nude (the Greeks seemed to do most things naked). Wrestling was extremely dangerous and although poking out your opponent's eyes was not allowed, it still happened from time to time. The Greeks also liked to box and used leather straps wrapped around each hand instead of gloves.

Competition Rules

Sports were big in Greece – the Olympic Games originated there. The Greeks believed that their gods wanted them to do lots of competitive exercise so they built huge stadiums for their Games. The Olympic Games was the most important sporting event and it was held every four years in honour of Zeus, the top god. The Panathenaic Games were also held every four years in Athens in honour of the goddess Athena.

Fighting Postponed

During times of war, the Games were so important that the Greeks called a two-month truce, during which time competitors and spectators could travel safely to Olympia, where the Games were held.

Waste Not Want Not

The ancient Greeks would start off each of the Games with a festival where an animal was sacrificed to Zeus. The animal's insides were "read" for omens, then all the athletes would have a big barbecue (to eat the animal which had been killed).

Born Head First

Athens was the largest city in Greece. It was named after the goddess Athena, who was born out of her father's head. He was the god, Zeus, who swallowed his pregnant wife whole and when the baby, Athena, was due, his head was cut open so she could be born (well, when you're a god or goddess you can do anything).

Greek Games

The Greeks liked to have fun and had plenty of festivals and drinking parties. They played a game called *cottabos*. To play cottabos all you had to do was to chuck what was left in your wine cup at a chosen target. The person who made the most direct hit with their wine dregs was the winner. You can see why they needed so many servants.

Knucklebones were played mainly by women. The bones were the ankle-bones of small goats and sheep which would be thrown into the air and caught on the back of the hand like the more modern game of "jacks". And the ancient Greeks probably invented board games. Games similar to snakes and ladders have been around for a couple of thousand years.

Play Time

Theatre developed in Greece and they had fantastic outdoor arenas which were *tiered* (each row higher than the one below, as in a modern-day stadium) so everyone could see and the sound of voices could carry right to the top tier without any artificial amplification.

Women weren't allowed to take part in plays so men took the female roles. They made up *dramas* about their gods and some of these plays are still put on today. The word *orchestra* means the flat bit in the middle of the arena.

Fitness and Fashion

The ancient Greeks liked to be clean and beautiful. Young men competed naked in the Games so they liked to keep their bodies fit and their skin oiled. Both men and women wore

finely woven clothes, and the women wore strips of cloth wrapped round their bodies for underwear. It wasn't fashionable to have a suntan so to keep out the sun both sexes would wear flat hats, which looked a bit like sundials on the tops of their heads.

Spartan Schooling

Sparta was a state in the south of Greece known for producing tough people. In school, corporal punishment was the norm – boys who didn't do well or pay attention were thumped!

Mini-Skirts

Girls didn't go to school in Sparta either, but they were encouraged to run and be active. They weren't expected to fight in wars but they were expected to keep themselves fit so that they could produce healthy babies. Spartan girls caused a few raised eyebrows because they wore their skirts much shorter than other Greek girls so they could do all that running.

Spears and Shields

The ancient Greeks had a pretty good army. The best kitted-out soldiers were called *hoplites*, which means "shield". They had to pay for their own spears and swords and armour, so the richer you were, the more likely you were to survive because you could pay for breastplates and leg guards. The leg guards of bronze were called *greaves* (like metal socks).

Married to Work

All Greek men were trained as soldiers for two years and could be called up in times of war. In Sparta though, boys were taken away at the age of seven to live and train with the army. Even when they were married they still lived in the barracks away from their wives and families.

Floating Bridge

The Persians (from what is now Iran) kept on trying to take the Greeks' land. In 490 BC, the Persians made a bridge of boats to cross a stretch of water called the Hellespont between Greece and Asia Minor. Their army was so huge that it took them seven days to walk across the boats to reach Greece.

There were loads of battles between the Greeks and the Persians. One of these was the Battle of Salamis – but they didn't fight each

other with long sausages! The Greeks won.

When the Greeks beat the Persians at Marathon in 490 BC, the Greeks suffered only 192 dead but the Persians lost 6,400 men. This was because the Greeks had far better tactics than the Persians

Decline and Fall

What happened to the Greek civilization? Alexander the Great defeated Persia and called himself King of Asia, which made the Greek Empire huge. But after Alexander died in 323 BC, it all went to pot. His greedy generals argued over and then split up the empire, which weakened it so much that it was ripe for a Roman takeover. And the rest is history!

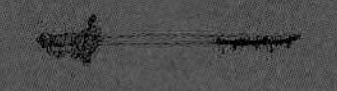

Gargantuan Greeks Quiz

1) What were *Linear A* and *Linear B*?
2) What was inside the Trojan Horse?
3) What was wrong with the Phoenician alphabet?
4) What was *cottabos*?
5) Who finally conquered the Greeks?

Answers

1) Types of early Greek writing or script.
2) Greek soldiers.
3) It didn't have any vowels.
4) A drinking game
5) The Romans.

CHAPTER FIVE

Rancid Romans

Elephant Man

The Romans built up a large empire over several centuries, which included most of Europe and the land around the Mediterranean Sea. The worst test of the Romans' power was Hannibal, the Carthaginian, who marched from Spain to Italy with all his elephants to attack the Romans.

The first war with Carthage was in 264 BC and battles raged between the two world powers for a further 23 years. A huge number of soldiers died but the Romans eventually beat the Carthaginians. By 146 BC Rome was the greatest power in the Mediterranean.

Pray Like Mad

Like the Greeks, the Romans had different gods for different things. They tried to keep the gods happy all the time – otherwise they believed that things would go pear-shaped for them. More often than not, Roman emperors became gods when they died.

Jupiter was the king of the gods (he was also known as "Best and Greatest"). Top goddess was Juno, Jupiter's wife, who was patron goddess of all women.

God Share

Good old Isis (the god with the bird's head) was also worshipped by the Romans, and so were quite a few of the Greek gods. One of these was Pan, who was half man, half goat (no kidding!). He was god of mountains and shepherds and other goaty things.

Mars was the god of war and Venus the goddess of love, beauty, and fertility (they certainly crammed 'em in). Bacchus was the god of wine and everyone looked forward to his festivals for some reason!

Making Sacrifices

Animals were killed on temple altars as sacrifices to the gods, especially the poor old cockerels and rams which were considered holy animals and therefore copped it the most.

When cows and other big animals were sacrificed they were killed and their insides would be taken out for the priest to examine the liver. If it wasn't very healthy or was badly formed, it was considered to be a bad omen. Sometimes humans would also be sacrificed. Yikes!

Persuasive Tactics

When the Romans bumped into the Christians, they thought the Christians would bring them danger because it was against their religion to sacrifice things to the gods or to worship any god but . . . well, the Christian god. So they threw a few of them to the lions to try to change their minds.

Water Works

The Romans were fantastic plumbers. They figured out such a brilliant system of waterways and drainage that nobody could come up with anything better until the Victorian era, hundreds of years later. However, they did use sponges on sticks instead of loo paper, hence the term "getting hold of the wrong end of the stick" (think about it . . .).

Bath and Laugh

A favourite thing to do in Roman times was to go down to the public baths. The "baths" weren't a swimming pool but a place where the Romans would go to bathe and exercise with their mates. They'd have a natter as they scrubbed each other's backs, but they must have been seriously greasy because instead of soap they used olive oil. Then they scraped off all the dirt and oil with a special tool called a *strigil*. Whoever cleaned the baths must've had their job cut out!

Looks Could Kill

The Romans regarded trousers as unmanly and preferred to wear tunics. For women, it was fashionable to have very pale faces with dark eyes and lips. They used a compound which contained white lead to achieve the look, and this slowly poisoned them.

Prepared to Die

They were a gory lot, the Romans. They loved blood sports and would crowd into the open-air arenas or *amphitheatres* to be entertained. Specially trained men (and sometimes women) called *gladiators* fought each other to the death for the entertainment of the crowds. Gladiators would begin their "performance" by shouting to the emperor in the audience: "We who are about to die salute you."

Many gladiators were slaves or criminals but they could sometimes earn their freedom if they were good at beating their opponents.

Net Work

A net man was a bloke who was really skilful with a big net. He'd fight a fully armed gladiator with only his net and a dagger, and would usually win. Net men also fought animals like bears, and sometimes more exotic animals such as tigers and rhinoceroses were captured and used. The floor of the arena was covered in sand to absorb the blood of the animal and human victims.

NET MAN

Curses!

The Romans had a way of getting back at people who'd done something horrible to them. All they had to do was to write a note to one of their gods on a *curse stone*, asking the god to do something nasty back to the person. They would then leave the stone in the temple and wait for it to work.

Historic Snapshot

When Mount Vesuvius blew its top in AD 79, the citizens of Pompeii were caught short and couldn't escape from the massive volcanic eruption. The hot lava buried everything several metres deep and "froze" the bodies in the act of whatever they were doing at the time, so historians have a pretty good idea of what life was like in a Roman town.

Marching Orders

Legions made up the main part of the Roman army that invaded Britain. Each legion had over 5,000 heavily armed and well-trained foot soldiers, who had to be Roman citizens. They sometimes had to march thirty kilometres (twenty miles) a day carrying huge weights on their backs of around forty kilos (ninety pounds) or more. They had to wear hobnailed shoes so they didn't wear out the leather with all that walking. They also wore bracelets in which they carried money.

Provincial Britain

The countries ruled from Rome were known as provinces. Britain became a province after the Roman army invaded in AD 43. The Romans built the 120-kilometre-long (75-mile) Hadrian's Wall to keep out the Caledonians, whom they hadn't managed to conquer.

Single Minded

Soldiers were not supposed to marry but many found a way of getting around that rule and had wives and children on the quiet. They often married women in the countries that they conquered (the women just couldn't resist the tall, dark Italians!). This helped to spread Roman customs throughout the empire.

Wicked Weapons
The Romans had some terrible tools for killing the enemy. They wore a short, wide sword and a dagger, as well as a spear or javelin. They also used an enormous crossbow called a *ballista*, which fired iron bolts at the enemy.

Roman soldiers wore armour made of metal "scales" which overlapped. Another type of armour, called *mail*, was made from small metal rings linked together.

When the Romans had won a battle, the emperor and his soldiers would parade the captured enemy leaders through the streets and then strangle them in front of the crowds.

Honk! Honk!

The Gauls were stopped in their tracks when they tried to raid Rome's Capitoline Hill in 390 BC. The Romans' holy geese made such a racket that the Romans woke up and escaped capture by the French fiends.

Odd Emperors

The Romans had lots of emperors even though Rome was supposed to be a *republic*, which meant that no one person was supposed to be in charge (that's why they wore "crowns" of laurel leaves instead of gold and jewels). Among the emperors was Caligula, who was a nasty piece of work. He went crazy and then he was murdered. Claudius (with the stutter) was a bit kinder, although he was the one who conquered Britain. Nero went mad too and supposedly started the great fire of Rome in AD 64 so he could rebuild the city. Then he killed himself, to the relief of a lot of people.

Off Colour

Only the emperor was allowed to wear purple because purple dye was made from a certain type of seashell and cost a fortune. Any ordinary person seen wearing purple clothes was likely to be slung in jail or executed as a traitor.

Landed Gentry

Even though the Romans were very civilized in some ways, life for people who worked in the countryside was tough. Most of the land was owned by the rich nobles who spent most of their time in the city, only coming to their large country houses at weekends or holiday time. So what's new?

Short Lives

Most people didn't live beyond the age of fifty and a lot of children died early from disease. Poor people would sometimes have to leave their new-born babies outside to die if they couldn't afford to feed them, or would sell their children as slaves.

The Romans had a little more knowledge than the Greeks about the workings of the human body but they still didn't have any anaesthetic or painkillers, and would perform operations with the patient still conscious. Aaargh! They prayed to the gods to heal them, especially to Aesculapius (all right if you can say it!), who was the god of healing, but, being sensible souls, they also tried to keep themselves healthy by eating lots of garlic and herbs.

A Day at the Races

One of the Romans' favourite pastimes was watching chariot racing. One racetrack in Rome could seat a quarter of a million people. Up to twelve chariots would race seven laps, a total of about eight kilometres (five miles), and spectators would bet on their favourite team.

The chariots consisted of either two-horse or four-horse chariots driven by a skilled charioteer. He had to be good because racing was extremely dangerous and the chariots often crashed into each other, resulting in the injury or death of the charioteer and sometimes the horses. Charioteers were mostly slaves, but could win enough money to buy their freedom and were often much admired.

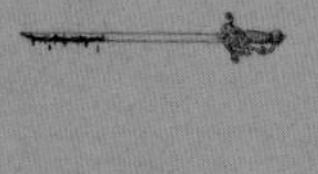

Barbaric Behaviour

What happened to the Roman empire? Around AD 230 they kept on being attacked by barbarians, so the Roman armies got stronger and stronger until they started fighting against each other in civil wars. In order to stop all the bickering, the emperor Diocletian divided the empire into four parts, each with its own ruler.

Christian Conversion

The emperor Constantine took over in AD 312 and built a new imperial capital, Constantinople (now the Turkish city of Istanbul), on the site of the Greek city of Byzantium a few years later. Under the rule of Constantine, who believed he was sent by the Christian God to rule the Roman empire, Romans had to convert to Christianity.

Brilliant Byzantine

The Roman empire was divided into east and west in AD 395. The eastern Roman empire defended itself from barbarian attacks and lasted for more than one thousand years. It became known as the Byzantine empire.

Huns by the Hundred

The western Roman empire didn't do so well. The barbarians were threatening from all sides. The worst of the barbarians, the Huns, were truly horrible. They came from central Asia and, led by Attila, they terrified all they met.

All Change!

In AD 476 the western Roman empire fell. Gaul became France, taken by the Franks; Britain was taken by the Angles and the Saxons, and Roman Britain became Saxon England.

Rancid Romans Quiz

1) Who was top god?
2) Name two animals which were considered "holy".
3) Why did soldiers wear bracelets?
4) What was a *strigil* used for?
5) What was a *curse stone* used for?

Answers

1) Jupiter.
2) Cockerels and rams.
3) To stash their cash.
4) For scraping dirt and oil off the skin during a bath.
5) For getting revenge on someone who'd harmed you.

CHAPTER SIX

Vicious Vikings

The Vikings were around for about 300 years, from the eighth to the eleventh centuries. They came from what we now call Scandinavia – from Sweden, Denmark, and Norway. They were also known as Danes and Norsemen. They raided loads of countries all over Europe and everyone was scared of them. Hardly surprising – the word "viking" means: taking a trip across the water to bring back some foreign booty (and beating up a few people to get it!).

Sailing Types

The Vikings were excellent at building boats and brilliant at sailing them. Their wooden ships were called *longships* and they were specially shaped so they could sail in very shallow water. When it was too shallow or narrow to have the sails up (like on a river or near a beach), they'd get out their oars and row the rest of the way.

This meant that they could land their ships almost on the beaches, so if they decided to raid your country they'd be on your doorstep before you knew it!

They looked pretty ferocious too. They wore chain mail or padded leather tunics and helmets, with noseguards and sometimes metal goggles to protect their eyes, so they probably looked like something out of *Mad Max*. They carried big, round, wooden shields, spears, and

double-edged iron swords as well as their axes, ready to do nasty things to anyone who tried to stop them.

Buried to the Hilt

If a Viking warrior was seriously rich and powerful, his sword would be encrusted with jewels or decorated with gold and silver. When he died, the warrior's weapons were often buried beside him. What a waste of money!

Warlike Mentality

The Vikings were warriors with attitude. Viking heaven was to be able to fight every day and they really thought it was OK to rob and kill people – as long as they were foreigners!

Breaking with Habit

One of the Vikings' earliest attacks on Britain was in AD 793, when they landed on the island of Lindisfarne. There was a castle there and an abbey, but the only inhabitants were monks. They killed some of the monks, stripped, beat, and insulted others, and captured another group to be taken back with them and sold as slaves. They kicked the place to bits and stole all the treasure. And all this was at a time when the Church was seen as sacred, and out of bounds for this kind of behaviour!

Not So Great Danes

The Vikings continued to do this sort of thing for the next 300 years, which didn't go down too well with the native Brits. They would land their boats and ride off to find the nearest villages, where they would then steal everything they could, kill the old people and children, and burn down what was left. They would chain up the young men and women and take them as slaves. Then they would disappear before the English army could get there.

Ragnar Revenged

King Aella of Northumbria decided to put a stop to this. When the alarmingly named Ragnar Hairy-Breeches and his men tried their gruesome games, King Aella was ready for them. He captured Ragnar and threw him in a snake pit. But Ragnar Hairy-Breeches' sons found out what had happened to him and captured King Aella. Without a second thought they broke his ribs apart and ripped out his lungs, which was a fairly standard thing to do.

Unready for Anything

There were loads of skirmishes between the Saxons (the Brits) and the Danes. Ethelred the Unready, who became the Saxon king at this time, decided to kill all the Danes who were living in England. On 13 November 1002 the massacre took place, with the Saxons burying adults alive and killing children violently.

After this, if a Dane was caught by a Saxon, his skin would be peeled off him while he was still alive and hung on the door of the nearest church.

You Can Take it with You

Rich Viking men were buried with their boats (imagine the size of the coffin!), together with their worldly possessions. Sometimes even their slaves were killed and buried with them when they died. Who'd have their job?!

The Arabs thought the Vikings were disgusting and filthy because they used the same bowl of water to wash their hands and faces, blow their noses, and to spit into, before passing it on to the next person. What's wrong with that?

The Thing Is . . .

Vikings got together at the *Thing*. Sounds like a horror movie, but it was actually the name of the place where people could have a good old beef about what was getting on their nerves. They'd sort out arguments there as well.

If a tiff couldn't be sorted by the Thing, the Vikings had something called *ordeals*, in which the two people who were having the barney would each try to prove that he was right. They did this by walking over red-hot coals, or doing something equally stupid and painful like trying to boil themselves alive, because they believed that the gods would look after them and if they were innocent they wouldn't get hurt. Doh!

Striking Vikings

Not all Vikings walked around in smelly sheepskins and hairy tunics. The rich Vikings were actually quite posh. They used tablecloths and silver goblets, and wore silk clothes. And if you were a posh Viking you ate white bread instead of the rough old brown stuff.

Even though they were big and tough, Viking men wore big brooches to hold their cloaks together.

To Cap it All

Disappointing though it may be, the Vikings didn't wear helmets with great big horns sticking out of them like in all the pictures. What they really wore were cute little round caps of leather or iron. How's that for spoiling their image!

Penetrating the East

The Vikings managed to sail across the Baltic Sea to Russia, then up the rivers right into the Byzantine empire and the city of Constantinople. They went on to Baghdad (which is now in Iraq). The Vikings were known as "Rus" by the eastern peoples which, funnily enough, might be where the term "Russian" came from (well, Scandinavia is very close to Russia – if you're a crow).

Exploring Outlaws

Many Viking explorers were men who had been exiled from their own lands. Erik the Red was exiled in 982 AD. He sailed to Iceland, but faced with the 1,830 metre (6,000 ft) ice cliffs of the Ingolfsfjeld Glacier he landed instead at what became known as "Erik's Island".

Erik the Red's son, Leif the Lucky, was also an explorer. He discovered America by accident when his ship went off course on a trip to Greenland.

Ropey Walrus

Vikings used walrus skins to make ropes for their ships. They skinned the walrus in a spiral, a bit like peeling an apple, to keep the skin in one long piece so that the rope didn't have any knots in it. (Did you hear the one about the walrus who didn't want to be killed? He said to the Viking: "Knot *me*, knot *me*!")

A Vine Place to Live

Around the year 1001, five hundred years before Christopher Columbus, Leif the Lucky became the first European to set foot on North America. He called America Vinland (Wineland) because he mistakenly thought that the ground was covered in grapevines. Nice thought, Leif.

The French Connection

The Vikings were bothering France so much that the king of France, Charles the Simple, gave them land as a deal to stop them invading. But, being Vikings, they gradually took more and more until the Viking king was more powerful than Simple Charles. The land was called Normandy after *men from the North* and was where the term *Normans* comes from.

Vicious Vikings Quiz

1) What was a Viking boat called?
2) What was the Thing?
3) What did the Vikings use to make ships' ropes?
4) Which country did the Vikings call Vinland (or Wineland)?
5) Where did the Vikings make their home?

Answers

1) A longship.
2) A public meeting place and a place to sort out arguments.
3) Walrus skin.
4) America.
5) Part of France, called Normandy.

CHAPTER SEVEN

Mucky Medievals

Blame it on the French

The Hundred Years War between France and England began in 1337, and it was the English soldiers fighting in France who brought the epidemic of plague known as the Black Death back with them (gotta blame someone!).

Very Black Death

In four years, from 1346 to 1350, twenty-five million people in Europe, over a third of the population, died from the Black Death. That's more than twice as many deaths in the same period during the First World War (when people were trying very hard to kill each other).

Rat Fever

The correct name for the Black Death was *bubonic plague*. The plague bacterium (*pasteurella pestis*, if anyone's interested) was carried by the fleas which infested the black rat. The process of infection was as follows: rat gets ill from infection and snuffs it. Exit flea, onto another rat or a human. Flea bites human and causes lumps called *buboes*. Human dies. Flea goes in search of fresh quarry. The name Black Death was nothing to do with black rats, but came about because of the black marks that formed on the skins of plague victims.

A Rat in Every Port

Plague was also spread from country to country by the rats on ships. As the ships stopped at ports around the world, rats went ashore to do a bit of shopping and spread a bit of plague. From the ports, the plague travelled inland and spread rapidly from Asia through Europe.

Fired Corpses

When the Mongols wanted to capture the city of Caffa in the Crimea, they fired plague-ridden dead bodies in giant catapults over the city.

walls to infect the people inside. It worked – the city became plague-ridden and the Mongols were able to conquer it.

Plague Ships

The downside of this was that people who continued to trade with the city caught the plague too. Some ships lost all their crew to the plague – there was literally no one left to steer the boat. Some countries banned ships that came from Caffa, knowing them to be death ships, so they stopped off in France instead and let the plague spread there.

Bubonic plague is still around today, but it can be controlled by antibiotics. The last occurrence of the disease was in Siberia in the early part of the twentieth century and *only* 60,000 people died then.

Dirty Debris

In medieval times people didn't mind having a few rats around: they helped clear up the mess on the floor after dinner. And no one really cared what they did with their waste. Sewage and rubbish were chucked into open drains which ran between the houses and ended up in the river, but not before the rats had had a pretty good chomp on it all. Mmmm!

Whipper Snappers

People thought that the Black Death was a punishment from God for their sins so they walked around whipping themselves to show that they were sorry for what they'd done. It's called *self-flagellation*, and apparently it doesn't half hurt.

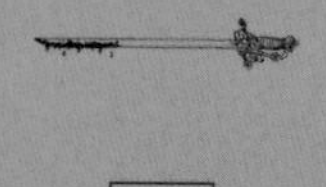

No Resistance

The population of Europe had increased enormously in the thirteenth century. Everyone was having babies, but there wasn't enough food to go round. Hungry, thin people couldn't fight off illness as well as those who were better fed, so the plague had a chance to get a good foothold.

Ignorant Docs

The *physicians* (doctors) and *apothecaries* (chemists) hadn't a clue what to do. They made up useless potions or extracted blood from people hoping that it would help, which of course it didn't. All that happened was that the people who'd had blood taken felt even worse than ever!

Twinkle, Twinkle

The physicians thought that the plague came from the stars, which in turn infected the rain. So they lit a load of bonfires and didn't let themselves get wet, but, not surprisingly, they still died of the plague. It wasn't until 500 years later that scientists discovered the bacterium that actually caused the Black Death.

One person who described life during the Black Death was a bloke called Geoffrey the Baker. He was a *chronicler*, which means he wrote everything down (so why he was known as the Baker is a bit of a mystery). He wrote that people became very suspicious of each other. For example, people in Gloucester wouldn't let the people from plague-ridden Bristol into their town because they thought their breath would infect them.

Let Down

After the Black Death people had a lot less faith in physicians and in the Church. They thought that doctors and priests had been pretty flaky and hadn't looked after them like they were supposed to. And they were right – a lot of priests just ran away, hoping to save their own skins.

Dash from Disaster

Those who survived the plague soon cottoned on to the fact that they could make some money out of it. Churchmen would charge a fortune to go into a parish to administer to the dying. Some people would just nick whatever was lying around (like land!) because there was no one to say, "Er, actually old chap, that's *mine*."

The labour force was reduced in number so

there were less peasants to do all the donkey work. That supposedly meant that they could at last call the tune and refuse to work unless they were given plenty of cash, but what really happened is that the peasants had to work harder than ever. This led, in 1381, to the Peasants' Revolt (the peasants really *were* revolting!), where they all rebelled and murdered landowners and clergy, who also happened to own a lot of land.

Other things that Happened in Medieval Europe . . .
Most people worked on the land and didn't have much money. In fact, the average lifespan of a peasant was twenty-five years. The lord of the manor owned the land and the peasants had to work it for him. In return they got a little bit of land to grow their own food, of which they had

to give a percentage to the lord as a tax.

The lord of the manor was usually the only one with a mill, which was used to grind corn for flour. He would often ban the use of hand mills so that all the peasants had to bring their grain to his mill and pay him a fee to grind it. Then he'd use the money to have big feasts and go out hunting all day, which seems a bit unfair. The peasants couldn't really do much about it though, because he was also the local judge! The lord of the manor was also a trained knight, so he could be called up in times of war to fight for king and country.

Once every blue moon, the peasants were invited to a big feast in the manor house, but only the lord of the manor had a proper bowl and cutlery. The rest of them had to make do with sharing bowls of food and eating with their fingers. Diners at the feast were told that,

if they needed to scratch themselves or pick their noses, they must do it with a piece of cloth, so that any grungy bits that got stuck to their fingers didn't go into the food. It's a good enough reason to take your own sandwiches!

Above the lords were the noblemen or barons, who would have their own mini-castles or forts. Noblemen were supposed to be loyal to their king but some of them had ideas above their station and behaved like kings themselves.

Vlad the Impaler was a Romanian baron who executed thousands of people by impaling them on stakes. He was such a horror that the

fictional vampire Dracula is generally thought to be based on him. He lived from 1430 to 1476 – which was a bit too long for some people!

Crime and Punishment

If a quarrel between two people couldn't be sorted by the court, the judge would allow something called "trial by combat". The two people concerned would arm themselves and fight with swords and axes, and they sometimes killed each other. Anyway, whoever won, won, so to speak.

There were some inventive punishments in medieval times. You could be dragged behind a galloping horse, put in the stocks, stretched out on a rack, whipped, hanged – in some cases for doing very little wrong, or at the whim of your lord or baron.

Burned at the Stake

People were burried alive a lot in medieval times. One particularly unfortunate group were women who were supposed to be witches but who were just ordinary people doing ordinary dull things. To test them for "witchiness" the would-be witches were *ducked*, which meant that they were strapped into a one-sided see-saw contraption and then lowered into a river or pond. When they'd been held under for several minutes they would be lifted back out. If they survived it proved that they were a witch so they would then have to be burned, because that's what you did to witches in those days. Needless to say, there were a lot of cases of mistaken identity. If they drowned they were deemed innocent, but it was a bit late by then.

Others were burned for their religious beliefs, like the Cathars of the twelfth century, who thought that the world was created by the devil. The Pope ordered them all to be burned alive on bonfires and wiped them out completely.

Holy Unpleasant

Most religious orders believed that the more they suffered, the closer they would get to God. Some monks lived in freezing conditions and ate very little, some went barefoot and wore hairy underclothes to make themselves really itchy and uncomfortable.

Sir Glance A Lot

Noblemen were encouraged to spend a lot of time at court so that the king could keep an eye on them. King Richard II took this a little too far. Courtiers were supposed to kneel or curtsey everytime the king looked in their direction. King Richard once sat for hours on his throne, just glancing around at the roomful of courtiers because he wanted to watch them bobbing up and down everytime his gaze fell on them. He was a bit of a kook anyway, so he was soon kicked out for this and other ridiculous behaviour.

Fairly Painful

If you had a toothache you didn't go to the dentist but down to the weekly market or fair where you could pay money to have your tooth pulled out with a pair of pliers and no painkillers. Sounds like no fun at all.

Change for the Better

Then in the fifteenth century everything changed and people began to focus on art and beauty. The strict cloak of religion was lifted and poets, writers, painters, and other artists emerged to celebrate humanity. The *Renaissance* (rebirth of art and culture) had begun.

Mucky Medievals Quiz

1) What was responsible for the Black Death?
2) Where did doctors think the plague came from?
3) What was the average lifespan of a peasant?
4) Where could you have bad teeth pulled out?
5) What was the name for the rebirth of art and culture in the fifteenth century?

Answers

1) The flea of the black rat, which carried the plague.
2) The stars.
3) Twenty-five years.
4) At the weekly market or fair
5) The Renaissance.

CHAPTER EIGHT

Aztecs with Attitude

The Aztecs lived in Mexico from around AD 1345 to AD 1520. Mexico is in Central America, which is the thin bit between North America and South America (Peru, Argentina, Brazil and all that lot).

The Aztecs originally came from further north. They had a god called Huitzilopochtli (that was easy for them to say). He was the sun god, and the Aztecs lugged a statue of him through hell and high water (well, mountains and deserts) until they came to Mexico where they settled.

Huitzilopochtli – let's just call him Huitz, shall we? – sent a sign to the Aztecs to start building on an island in the middle of a lake. They built a city there and called it "Place of the Fruit of the Prickly Pear" which luckily in Aztec language is a much shorter name, although a bit more difficult to pronounce: Tenochtitlan. This city became the capital of the Aztec empire, and in its heyday it housed nearly a quarter of a million people.

The Aztec ruler or king was called the Tlatoani. These blokes soon became a bit too big for their boots and tried to pretend that they were superhuman. They wore big feather headdresses and sometimes masks to make them look the part.

Identity Crisis

One of the king's most important sidekicks was the Ciuacoatl, which means "Snake Woman" – except that he was a man. Funny that! He obviously had a double identity crisis. He was the person in charge of running the place, a bit like the Prime Minister, while the Tlatoani sat around chatting to his many wives or ordering his shedloads of servants around.

Triple Time

The Aztecs had three different calendars: one had 260 days, another had 365 days like ours, and yet another had 584 days. These calendars all ended at the same time every 104 years. This was when the Aztecs thought it would be the end of the world.

Prickly Beer

The Aztecs had pretty strict rules. You couldn't drink alcohol unless you were over thirty years old and even then you weren't allowed to knock it back unless you were really old or ill (makes you wonder how many of them pretended to be ill just so they could have half a lager). Mind you, the beer was made from cacti, so perhaps people weren't that keen anyway.

All the people, except for the king of course, had to do as they were told. If they did something wrong they had their house knocked down, and if they did it again there was no second chance – they would be killed.

Fierce Fighters

The Aztecs were warriors first and foremost and liked nothing better than to go and conquer a

DON'T MESS WITH US!

city belonging to another tribe. They had some fearsome weapons: a cudgel with bits of volcanic glass sticking out of it, as well as spears and axes, so it wasn't a good idea to argue with them.

Human Sacrifice

Once the Aztecs had conquered an enemy they could demand taxes, or *tributes* as they were known – anything from basic foodstuffs to treasures. The other rather nastier reason for lording it over other tribes was so that the Aztecs could capture and use them as human sacrifices to their gods, rather than using their own people.

Lucky Charms

When a warrior was feeling a bit cowardly, or was worried that he wouldn't do so well in his next battle, he would dig up the grave (or grab the body before it got to the grave) of a woman who had died in childbirth. If he cut off her hair and fingers and stuck them onto his shield, it was supposed to bring the warrior good luck. (Yeeuch!)

Respected Ghouls

Women who'd died giving birth to their children were obviously highly thought of, but people were also frightened of their ghosts, which were supposed to haunt the streets. Hardly surprising. The poor girls were probably looking for their fingers!

Dying for Work

Parents were very strict with their children. From the age of around five years, kids had to work to help their families, doing jobs such as cleaning, farming, and fishing. Another thing that was left to children was collecting a certain type of insect from cactus plants to make a red dye called *cochineal*.

Harsh Treatment

If children were naughty or disobedient, they were given punishments like being held over a fire and made to breathe the smoke from burning chilli peppers. Bit over the top for not tidying your room, eh? During droughts and famine children were often sold into slavery rather than staying at home and starving to death. What a choice!

Playing Ball

Every Aztec city had a Ball Court. This was a long rectangular area with another rectangular box at either end with a stone floor and high stone walls, a bit like an enclosed letter "I".

The Ball Game was the Aztecs' favourite sport. It was a bit like a cross between volleyball and basketball, except that the ball was small and heavy, made of hard, solid rubber. Another big difference was that players weren't allowed to use their hands, only their hips and knees, to get the ball through a stone ring placed very high up on the wall.

Players wore padded clothes to try to minimize their injuries but it was still a really dangerous game to play, so there was a lot of body swerving going on. The Aztecs would enjoy watching it – until someone scored a goal and then they'd all leg it. Why? Because the player who scored was allowed to take all the possessions (including the clothes!) of the spectators.

Unhelpful Remedies

When the Aztecs got sick, they thought that evil spirits had taken over their body. The witch doctor would make them up a potion of really poisonous plants and herbs, then say a few spells. Sometimes, if they hadn't already died from whatever disease they had, patients would keel over once the doctor had been.

Worth Dying Well

When Aztecs died they were usually *cremated* (burned) and their ashes put into a pot. Sometimes they were wrapped in cloth and buried with some of their possessions. They believed that if you got killed in a horrible way in this life, or you died in childbirth, then you would be OK in the next life. If you'd had an easy life, you could expect to find yourself floating around for ages until you met your end at *Mictlan*, which was "a place of dark emptiness". So an easy life meant a tough afterlife – not a pleasant thought.

Reptile Rags

There were other gods apart from old Huitz, whom we've mentioned earlier. One of them was his mum, Coatlicue. She was the earth goddess and her name meant "Serpent Skirt" because she always wore a skirt of poisonous snakes. (If she had the legs for it, why not?)

Have a Heart

There was also Tlaloc, the god of water and rain. The Aztecs thought that if Tlaloc got cross he would flood them, so they kept him happy by throwing him fresh human hearts. The other thing Tlaloc could do was to stop the rain completely, causing a drought. To prevent this, the priests would kill children. They believed that the more the children cried, the more rain would fall. (And you thought it was tough when you got extra homework!)

Second Skin

Xipe Totec was the god of spring. He needed carefully selected men to be killed, skinned, and draped over his statue in order to ensure that new crops would grow. Another god was Xochipilli, which meant "flower prince". He was only a young bloke but on all his statues he had the face of a dead man. Creepy or what?

Lord of Nowhere

Not all the Aztecs believed in all these different gods: some thought there was only one god and that was – wait for it – the Lord of Nowhere. They didn't build any statues or make any drawings of this particular god. Why? Presumably because he was Nowhere to be seen. Geddit?

Bloodthirsty Huitz

Remember Huitzilopochtli was the god of the sun? Well, the Aztecs believed that he needed to be fed constantly with human blood or he'd make everything seriously bad – like no sun, which meant there would be no warmth or light, nothing would grow and everyone would die. Oh, lighten up, Huitz!

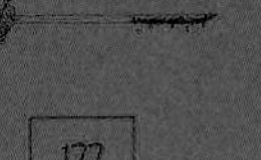

Skull Rack

With all these bloodthirsty gods to appease, the Aztecs needed a steady supply of sacrificial victims. As we know, they used criminals or slaves captured from neighbouring cities, but when they'd run out of these they'd use ordinary citizens and children. There was a skull rack where they put all the heads of the people who'd been sacrificed. Nice.

High Church

Aztec temples could be nearly 90 metres (300 feet) high, with steep steps all the way up to the altar. This was where the sacrifices were made to the gods.

Unfair Advantage

The victim was tied to a post and made to fight four fully armed men at once. To make it fair (not!), the victim was allowed to arm himself with wooden weapons. When he had been killed (which is what usually happened), the Aztecs carried him up to the temple altar and cut out his heart with a special, prettily decorated knife which was used for doing just that.

When the gods were really angry, the Aztecs didn't bother to kill the sacrifices first, but cut them open and pulled out their heart while they were still alive (although not for long).

Unprincipled Priests

The priests were a weird lot. In their day jobs they were lawyers and scribes and "respectable" people like that, but they lost it completely when they did their stint as priests. Priests and priestesses painted their faces black, let their hair get all filthy and tangled, and didn't wash so that they stank.

They stayed awake for nights on end and the lack of sleep, plus the fact that they often took mind-altering drugs, made them demented – not to mention all the gross things they had to do in the sacrifice ceremonies. The temples stank too, from all the dead bodies and blood. It was a bit different from popping down to your local church on a Sunday and listening to the organ play while the vicar drones on.

Hair of the Dog

The Aztecs bred a special kind of dog that had very little hair and kept them as pets, until it was time to eat them! Other than that they ate frogs, locusts, ants . . . the usual sort of thing.

Water Garden

The Aztecs created floating gardens around the edge of lakes, which were known as chinampas. They made a framework from twigs and reeds, filled it with fertile mud from the lake bottom and sank it. The roots from the fruit and vegetables they grew helped to hold it in place. Then – have you had your breakfast? – human "waste" was collected from toilets in the towns and from the sides of the road. It was spread over the soil to help the plants to grow. Another tomato, anyone?

Wheely Unnecessary

For all their engineering skills, the Aztecs had no wheels. They didn't use carts, probably because they didn't have any horses or oxen or donkeys to pull them (and the hairless dogs would have been pretty useless in this instance). So they paddled everywhere by canoe, or walked, carrying their loads on their backs like mules.

Meaningful Hair

Single girls wore their hair loose and flowing, while married women put theirs up. Unmanly young men (those who hadn't yet killed anyone in battle!) had to leave a bit of their hair long to show that they were wimps.

Warriors wore a cute little topknot to show what men they were!

Foreign Invasion

The Spanish *Conquistadores* (conquerors) invaded in 1519 and eventually conquered most of Central and South America, mainly because it was so rich in gold and silver and they wanted it. At first they demanded huge ransoms of gold and silver, pretending that they'd leave the Aztecs alone if they coughed up. They melted

down all the precious metal artefacts so they could get more gold and silver into the holds of their ships. (The stories of Spanish galleons full of treasure come from this era – they nicked most of it from the Aztecs.)

Anyway, the Spanish lied about going away if the Aztecs gave them all their gold. Hernando Cortés was the Spanish leader who eventually captured the ruling city of the Aztecs. The first time he tried he was beaten back, even though the Aztecs were pretty frightened by this half man, half creature (man on horseback) that they'd never seen before.

Caught by Cortés

Cortés returned two years later. The Aztecs were seriously disadvantaged by their lack of both horse and gun power and Cortés' army massacred them. The Spanish destroyed the "Place of the Fruit of the Prickly Pear" because its name was too long (only joking!) and built their own city on top of it. This became the capital of modern Mexico, Mexico City.

Spanish Records

It was a Spanish chap or, should we say, "hombre", called Mendoza who ordered records to be kept of what the Aztecs were all about. If it wasn't for him no one would know much about them at all (did someone say, "Good, one less thing to learn . . ."?). Unfortunately – for historians, at any rate – a bunch of stories that were drawn by the Aztecs (they used pictures instead of words) was burned by some rather dim Spanish missionaries who thought they were evil.

No More Aztecs

Mexico itself became a Spanish colony in 1535. Spanish settlers helped themselves to the Aztecs' gear and land, and made the Aztecs work for them (those that they hadn't killed already). And that, sadly, was the end of the Aztec civilization.

Aztecs with Attitude Quiz

1) What was the name given to the Aztec ruler?
2) How many different calendars did the Aztecs have?
3) What is cochineal?
4) What were *chinampas*?
5) How could you tell if an Aztec woman was married?

Answers

1) The Tlatoani.
2) Three – one of 260 days, one of 365 days and one of 584 days.
3) A red dye made from tiny insects.
4) Gardens created on or around lakes.
5) She always wore her hair up on her head.

CHAPTER NINE

Toxic Tudors

Wars of the Roses

The *Tudors* came to power in England when they won the ongoing fight between the House of York and The House of Lancaster (the Tudors). This was known as the Wars of the Roses, not because they hit each over the head with prickly flowers, but because each side had a rose on its flag.

Dull Hal

Henry Tudor beat King Richard II (York) at the Battle of Bosworth in 1485 and became King Henry VII. Apart from being the first in the Tudor line, Henry VII was dull and boring so we'll skip him and go on to Henry VIII.

Dead Man's Shoes

Henry VIII was the second son of Henry VII, and therefore not heir to the throne. He only became king when his older brother Arthur died. Then Henry married Arthur's wife, Catherine of Aragon, apparently at the insistence of his brother just before he died.

Potty Pains

Even though Henry ruled at the time of the Renaissance, people were still stuck with some grotty habits left over from mucky medieval times. Most people pooed into chamber pots and then chucked the contents out of the window, all over anybody who happened to be walking in the street below.

The royals were a little more civilized (they could afford to be!). Henry VIII used to sit on a velvet padded box which had a potty inside. He always had a servant with him when he went. The servant was called the Yeoman of the Stool. Phwaw! What a job!

Swaddled, Not Mollycoddled

Henry and Catherine had six babies but only Princess Mary survived, although they did have a son who died after six weeks. It's not surprising that one in three children didn't survive into adulthood. Their parents did strange things to them, like keeping them *swaddled* or wrapped tightly in cloth for the first few months of their lives. This was supposed to keep them still and to make sure that their bones grew straight.

Not Long in the Tooth

When babies were cutting their teeth, they had a revolting mixture rubbed on their gums. It contained hare's brains, goose fat, and honey. Or they'd be given a horse's tooth to chew on. It's enough to make anyone dribble!

After an Heir

Anyway, back to Henry. Although he had an *illegitimate* (born outside marriage) son by his mistress, he was desperate for a boy who would be able to take over his throne. Henry realized that he would have to marry someone else to get the son he so badly wanted, which meant he had to divorce Catherine so he could marry again.

Desperate Measures

Catherine of Aragon was Catholic and for her, divorce was forbidden. Henry had to go to great lengths to get rid of Catherine so he could take another wife. Finally, after the Pope had refused to dissolve his marriage, Henry split the Church of England from the Roman Catholic Church, and made himself head of the English Church so he could do what he liked. He then divorced Catherine of Aragon.

Fall from Grace

At that time, Cardinal Wolsey was head of the Catholic Church in England and was also one of Henry's favourites, which caused much jealousy in the rest of the court. Wolsey would do anything for the king, so when Henry wanted to divorce Catherine he asked the cardinal to get permission from the Pope. The Pope flatly refused and Cardinal Wolsey fell out of favour with Henry.

Wolsey tried to get back into the king's good books by giving him his own palace, Hampton Court, as a gift, but it was no use. From that time onwards, his days were numbered and his enemies began to plot against him. He was asked to come to London to answer charges of *treason* (crime against king and country) but died on the journey there.

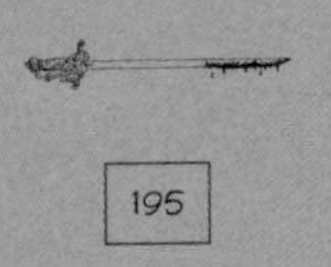

Dissolving the Monasteries

Henry decided that the Church was too rich and ordered the Dissolution of the Monasteries, which means that he had most of them burned or pulled down and took all their wealth.

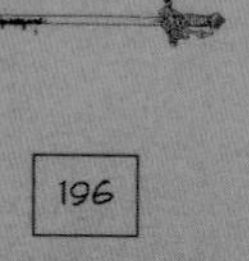

Wrong Sex

Now that Henry had got rid of Catherine he was free to wed Anne Boleyn, and did so not long after. Anne gave birth to a baby girl, Elizabeth (who would become Elizabeth I).

Kinder Cut

Henry was so miffed that he'd got yet another girl child that he had Anne Boleyn's head chopped off in 1536. Normally an axe was used, but Henry brought in a special executioner from France, who struck off Anne's head with a sword. How kind of Henry. She was known as Anne of a Thousand Days because that's how long she lasted after she married the king.

A Son at Last

Not long after Anne was out of the picture, Henry married Jane Seymour who he'd had his eye on for a while, but she died in childbirth a year later. Never mind that – Henry at last had a son, Edward.

Unlucky in Love

Henry was a bit worried that he wasn't doing too well on the wife front, so he left it a bit longer before marrying Anne of Cleves in 1540. Before he asked Anne to marry him he'd only seen a portrait of her and he thought he fancied her, but when it was too late he realized that Anne wasn't as pretty as her picture! He divorced Anne in the same year and almost immediately married Catherine Howard.

Faithless Then Headless

Now Catherine Howard was a bit of a naughty girl and started seeing someone on the side while she was married to Henry. In 1542, Henry lopped off her head as well for being unfaithful to him, and married Catherine Parr. She, amazingly, outlived Henry by a year.

Not Such a Bad Chap

Henry wasn't just a womanizer. He was a strong ruler and did some good things for England. One of them was to build a great navy, which was useful for protecting the country and for going off to discover foreign lands.

The *Mary Rose*

Henry had the warship, the *Mary Rose*, built in 1510. In 1545, the English coast was attacked by a fleet of French warships. Henry went to watch his navy do their stuff and defeat the French. The *Mary Rose* was there with all her gunports open ready to fire. Suddenly the ship flipped onto her side, tipping all the soldiers into the sea. Around 750 drowned. The *Mary Rose* was salvaged nearly 400 years later, in 1982, and is now on display in Portsmouth, the port off which she sank.

Unfit to be King

In his last few years Henry was a fat old couch potato. He had a terrible diet – he ate masses of meat and game and very few vegetables. He had terrible *gout* (a disease often linked with too much rich food) and was so overweight that he couldn't do any exercise, even walking, because it was too painful.

Quick Succession

Henry VIII died in 1547 and his son Edward became King Edward VI at the age of nine. The throne went to Mary, his half-sister, when Edward died six years later in 1553. Elizabeth ruled from 1558.

Moving Swiftly On . . .

When Elizabeth I came to the throne, she moved her court and courtiers around the country a lot, staying in other palaces and large houses belonging to nobles. The main reason for doing this was that after the court had stayed in a place for a while, it would need a good clean. There could be hundreds of people staying in one palace at a time and there were no sewers. The palaces became full of rubbish and got so stinky that after a few weeks it was definitely time to move on.

Anything Else, Sir?

Barbers in Tudor times didn't only cut hair. They cut off other things that people didn't need, like mouldy toes and other bits of body that had gone rotten, and stuck knives into boils to let the pus out. (Ugh!) That's why the poles outside barbershops were red and white – to represent blood and bandages.

Fag-Ash Liz

Tobacco was brought from the Americas and smoking became fashionable and was believed to be healthy. People would puff away (even Queen Elizabeth) because they thought it would help protect them from the plague.

Scent to Protect

The Tudors also thought that if they carried around a *pomander*, a ball with lots of smelly stuff in it like dried flowers and herbs, it would stop them from getting nasty diseases from other people.

Royal Flush

Elizabeth I supposedly had a good sense of smell, although she didn't seem to notice that she had really bad breath (she eventually lost all her teeth from eating too many sweets!). Nevertheless, she was responsible for the first flushing loo. She claimed she couldn't bear the smell of the palace lavvies so she had a flushing one invented for her by Sir John Harington. Perhaps that's where the expression "going to the John" came from?

End of the Line

Elizabeth I had no children and the Tudor line ended with her death in 1603. The Scottish king, James VI (at that time England and Scotland were separate kingdoms), became King James I of England, the first in the Stuart line of English monarchs.

Toxic Tudor Quiz

1) What was the war between the Yorks and the Lancasters called?
2) Which man of the Church was Henry VIII's favourite?
3) How many of his wives did Henry have executed?
4) Which Tudor ship sank spectacularly in 1545?
5) What did the barbershop's red-and-white poles stand for?

Answers

1) The Wars of the Roses.
2) Cardinal Wolsey.
3) Two – Anne Boleyn and Catherine Howard.
4) The Mary Rose.
5) Blood and bandages.

CHAPTER TEN

Revolting Revolution

From the mid-eighteenth to the mid-nineteenth centuries there were a lot of revolutions. A revolution happens when people, usually the poor ones of the country, decide that enough is enough and overthrow the government or king or queen who rules them.

From Worse to Bad

Revolutions usually happen not when things are really, really bad (which is what you would expect), but when things have improved a bit and people realize that there's more to life than working your socks off and then giving all your money to someone who's got more than you already. This bit is all about the French Revolution.

Louis the Pig

At the time of the French Revolution, the king of France was Louis XVI (that's Louis the Sixteenth for those non-Romans among us). He wouldn't say boo to a goose (well he probably would, but not very loudly), and he couldn't control all his noblemen, who were taxing the poor and spending a lot of money on themselves. Louis was also a bit of a pig. Someone very close to him in the royal household reported that one day for breakfast he had "four cutlets, a chicken, a plateful of ham, half a dozen eggs in sauce, and a bottle and a half of champagne". What a porker!

Bastille Day

On 14 July 1789, an angry mob attacked a big prison in Paris called the Bastille and let out all the prisoners. The French Revolution had begun! Suddenly the aristocracy weren't in charge any more and the common people had freedom to speak out against their oppression.

Chop 'n' Plop

The only trouble was that, after years and years of being told what to do, power went to people's heads, which meant that a lot of other people ended up losing theirs. The favourite instrument for removing heads was called the guillotine. It was a tall contraption with a sharp blade which was dropped from a height onto the neck of the victim. The head would roll into a basket (called laughingly – by those who weren't having their heads cut off – "sneezing into the basket"). The head would then be held up to the applause of the crowds.

Party Dip

In 1793 they executed Louis XVI and crowds of people turned up to watch because a lot of people hated the king and all he stood for.

When Louis' head was held up to the crowd, everyone rushed forward with handkerchiefs and bits of cloth to soak up the royal blood to keep as a memento.

Off with her Head!

Marie Antoinette was the king's wife and people didn't like her much either. She spent heaps of money on clothes and jewellery and didn't give a monkey's about the poor people. When they complained of having no bread she is supposed to have said, "Let them eat cake!" So she had her head chopped off too!

Gruesome Grannies

There were a bunch of women who used to go to the guillotine every day to watch the executions.

They'd take their knitting and some chairs to sit on and make a day of it. They were called the "Knitting Club" or "The Furies of the Guillotine" because as well as knitting they would also spit and shout insults at the people who were about to lose their heads.

The guillotine was tested for the first time at a prison in Paris called Bicêtre. They tried it out on the prisoners until it did the job properly. Bicêtre was the worst prison to end up in because prisoners were tortured and kept chained to each other, and not many people came out of it alive.

The Terror

From 1793 to 1794, there was a period called *The Terror*. It was when the people who'd taken charge of France after the king was beheaded decided to kill a whole lot more people for not very good reasons. If you looked a bit too rich or noble, or they thought that you didn't support them, they'd haul you off to prison and then cut off your head.

Do it Yourself

People were frightened all the time and things got so bad that some preferred to be dead rather than live with all the fear and bloodshed. If they couldn't quite bring themselves to commit suicide, all they had to do was to walk out into the street and shout "*Vive le Roi!*", or "Long Live the King!" Anyone who supported the king was seen to be a traitor so it wasn't long before they'd be hauled off to the guillotine.

Robespierre's Calendar

It was a bloke called Robespierre who headed up The Terror. He started off OK with some good ideas about how to help the poor, but soon got a bit over-excited and started to execute his old schoolmates and other unfriendly stuff. He even changed the calendar and made a week ten days long instead of seven (imagine going to school during those times!). Sunday was the only day off and it was the only day that the guillotine stopped working. Robespierre also renamed the months and gave them names like the *Month of Snow* and the *Month of Flowers*.

Although a lot of the rough stuff went on in the capital, Paris, there was also trouble in the rest of France. In a town called Nantes, the citizens refused to accept the Revolutionary Government which had taken over from the king, so they all had to be executed. It would have taken too long to guillotine them one by one, so all the inhabitants of the town were taken on a barge into the middle of the river and the barge was sunk.

Robespierre himself got executed in 1794 and things settled back down, but the French didt't have a king to rule them again until after the fall of Napoleon, 1814-5.

Revolting Revolution Quiz

1) Who was king of France at the time of the French Revolution?
2) What was the French instrument of execution called?
3) What was the name of Louis XVI's wife?
4) Who were known as the Knitting Club?
5) Who was responsible for The Terror of 1793–4?

Answers

1) Louis XVI.
2) The guillotine.
3) Marie Antoinette.
4) The women who sat watching the executions.
5) Robespierre.

CHAPTER ELEVEN

Vile Victorians

Kissin' Cousins

When she was twenty years old, Queen Victoria's parents arranged for her to marry her German cousin, Prince Albert of Saxe-Coburg-Gotha – what a mouthful!

A Decent Proposal

Apparently, cousins Bert and Vicky weren't too keen on the idea at first, but Victoria went ahead and asked Albert for his hand, because no man is allowed to propose to a queen. He said yes (because he'd been told to). They ended up with nine children so they must've liked each other a bit!

Black Widow

When Prince Albert died of typhoid in 1861, Queen Victoria didn't appear in public for ten years after his death, and even after that she still wore black for the rest of her life to show she was in mourning.

Christmas Tradition

But it is thanks to Albert that we have Christmas trees because he insisted (before he died, that is) on the German tradition of having a tree in the house at Christmas to hang chocolate coins on and to stuff presents underneath.

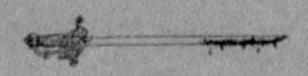

Revolting Industry

The Industrial Revolution wasn't a war, although many people were against it. It's the name given to a time when machines were first invented for doing things that people used to do by hand, like grinding corn, spinning wool, and weaving cloth.

Most of these machines were powered by steam. The machines were sometimes going all day and night so the Victorians had to burn a lot of coal to make enough steam to power them.

The air got so smoky that all the buildings turned black and lots of people had breathing problems caused by pollution.

Unguarded Moments

But the worst thing was when people got caught in the machines because they didn't have any safety guards. The doctors would have to chop off an arm or a leg (or whichever bit had got mangled) without any anaesthetic – the stuff that puts you to sleep before an operation.

Dirty Docs

Also, doctors still weren't completely clued up about surgical procedure and hadn't worked out that they should wash their hands and use antiseptic until around the mid-1800s, so many operations resulted in the death of the patient from infection.

Political Stink

People generally still didn't know much about hygiene. Cholera and typhoid – caused mainly by drinking dirty water – were common. The River Thames got so filled with sewage and rubbish that, in 1886, MPs had to leave the Houses of Parliament because the stench was so bad!

Child Labour

Coal had to be mined from under the ground, of course, and somebody had to do it. The Victorians thought nothing of putting children to work in the mines, even kids as young as five. If you were scared of the dark, hark luck, because there wasn't much light down a coal shaft. They didn't have torches because they hadn't been invented, so children (and grown-ups) would be working almost blind for about thirteen hours a day. The youngest ones worked as "trappers", which meant they had to sit in the dark in a cold, cramped space and open and close the "traps", or ventilators, which allowed the fresh air into the mine.

Intrepid Explorer

Women weren't allowed to vote and didn't have equal rights with men. If they did a similar job

to a man they would be paid less. Nevertheless, there were some pretty amazing women around in Victorian times. One of them was Mary Kingsley, an explorer, who used to wander around deepest, darkest Africa, and wouldn't be seen dead without her trademark trendy hat. She didn't take any nonsense from man-eating (or in this case, woman-eating) crocodiles or hippos – she just gave them a clout with her brolly.

Determined Doctor

Another cool lady was Sophia Jex-Blake. As she was a girlie, she wasn't allowed to study medicine, but she made so much fuss that eventually they let her into university. She passed all her exams but it wasn't until 1894 that women were allowed to be doctors, so Sophia had to wait twenty-five years before she could get a job.

Ashes to Ashes

The English cricket team played the first Test Match against the Australians in 1877, and the

Australians won! "That's the end of English cricket", they thought, so they set fire to the *bails* (the bits of wood on top of the wickets) and shoved the leftover ashes into a box. This is why the cricket trophy which is still played for today is called The Ashes. Fancy making such a fuss about a pile of burned wood.

Easy Rider

You'd get a sore bum cycling around on a *penny farthing*. The wheels had no rubber tyres and were made of wood. Hardly surprising they were called boneshakers! Then good old John Dunlop invented the blow-up tyre in 1888 and cycling really took off.

Itsy-bitsy Crinoline

Women kept all their clothes on when they went swimming – sometimes even their corsets, which of course had to be rustproof – because they thought that bare bits like knees and tummies were rude. In fact, any kind of bare legs were rude to the Victorians – they even covered up the chair and table legs in their homes!

It's a Cover-up!

Men weren't much better. They wore a sort of pyjama-type thing which went down to their knees and buttoned at the neck, so you couldn't see their rude bits either.

Off Their Heads

Ever heard the expression "Mad as a Hatter"? Well, there's a good reason for it. Hatters (people who made hats, funnily enough) used to rub mercury, which is poisonous, into the felt material they were using to make the hats. The poison would get into the hatters' blood through their fingertips and often cause them to go bonkers.

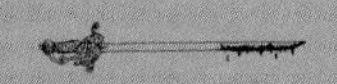

No Alternative

Children from poor families worked in factories, sometimes for as long as fourteen hours a day. For people who were really, really poor or had been thrown out of their homes by their own families, there was something called the workhouse. This was a cold, inhospitable place with very little food to eat, which was really no better than a prison. However, it made the government feel better because they thought they were looking after the less well-off, so it served a purpose.

Read All About It

In the early 1800s only very rich people were *literate* – able to read and write. One hundred years later, 90 per cent of people in Britain were literate.

Wed then Dead

When Hitler realized he would lose the war, he married his girlfriend of several years, Eva Braun. The next day they both committed suicide. No one seems sure how they did it, because their bodies were burned to avoid recognition, but it seems that Hitler shot himself and Eva took poison.

However, some people think that Hitler and Eva Braun pretended to die but escaped and lived a long time after the Second World War ended. A truly alarming thought.

Suspicious Spies of the Second World War Quiz

1) What did Hitler have a weakness for?
2) Which people were used by both sides to gather information?
3) Name three ways of passing on a secret message.
4) Name the German coding machine and the British code-breaker.
5) What poison were spies given to take if they need to commit suicide?

Answers

1) Chocolate cake.
2) Waiters and hotel workers.
3) Roll it in a cigarette; write it on your body in invisible ink; put it into a secret hole in the wall.
4) Enigma and Ultra.
5) Cyanide.